M000283710

# THE HOUSE
# THAT JACK BUILT

# THE HOUSE
# THAT JACK BUILT

## AND THE PEOPLE WHO LIVED THERE

### JAMES WYNN

First published 2007 by Aurum Press Limited
7 Greenland Street
London NW1 0ND
www.aurumpress.co.uk

Copyright © 2007 James Wynn

The moral right of James Wynn to be identified as the author of this
work has been asserted by him in accordance with the Copyright,
Designs and Patents Act 1988.

All rights reserved. No part of this book may be reproduced or utilized
in any form or by any means, electronic or mechanical, including
photocopying, recording or by any information storage and retrieval
system, without permission in writing from Aurum Press Ltd.

A catalogue record for this book is available from the British Library.

ISBN-10:  1 84513 282 3
ISBN-13:  978 1 84513 282 8

10 9 8 7 6 5 4 3 2 1
2011 2010 2009 2008 2007

Designed and typeset in Arrus by Robert Updegraff
Printed and bound in Great Britain by Cromwell Press, Trowbridge, Wiltshire

*For Anna and my girls, Abby and Juy*

# Acknowledgements

I would like to thank my agent, Lizzy Kremer of David Higham Associates, who never stopped believing in this book; Martin Crocker, my friend and critic whose comments and humorous additions were invaluable; and my editor, Piers Burnett, who has helped me round the final lap with patience, good humour and considerable skill. But there would have been no one to thank, no book to write if it had not been for Anna and the endless hours she spent reworking the early drafts. I see now, having finally finished, that nothing would have happened without her – thank you.

# Contents

# Escape from the City

I HAD ALWAYS WANTED a home, not just a place to live. You
know things aren't quite right when the Hammersmith Bridge
becomes the gateway to Arcadia. The weekends were the worst.
Since we had just had our second daughter the need to get out of
the city at weekends during the summer had become ever more
urgent. Like so many families we craved more space. We had
moved to the city because that was where all the interesting work
was but now, ten years later, our life was full of buggies and those
difficult machines for sterilising baby's milk. Driving back into
London after another escape we would rehearse yet again all the
excellent reasons why we needed to stay in the city. Neither of us
had been born in London but over the years we had persuaded ourselves that life was so much more exciting there. These arguments
(and all their close cousins) had always worked moderately well.
But now it suddenly seemed clear to both of us that we needed to
stop talking about moving out of London one day – with children
aged four and two, the day was now or it was not at all.

And so like many before us we joined the traffic jam that opti-
mistically calls itself the Westway and set off in search of more
space, more garden and, perhaps most significantly, more peace.
There are few more powerful dreams than the English countryside
variety – full of sepia-tinted lazy days in the garden, walks along
river meadows and the sound of skylarks (or is it children?) war-
bling as the sun dips behind the golden fields. This scene is sometimes followed by another in which everyone has been joined by a
matching set of children who have jumped out of a magazine. This
particular version is available in clean, sharp-edged, primary colours.
In it, the children tumble over each other like puppies and jump in

slow motion over sheaves of bright yellow corn. Sadly but inevitably even the best movies have to finish, the soundtrack (a haunting modern version of Vivaldi's *Four Seasons*) falls away and the picture fades tastefully to black.

Back in the real world of the self-employed, we felt we needed to stay within striking distance of London and so worked our way steadily westwards: first Winchester (too close to London) then Salisbury (the sepia images changed suddenly to black and white) and finally to Bath. We wanted our country clean, dry and pretty.

As we dipped down from the southern edge of the Cotswolds and saw Bath spread out beneath us, it seemed that our dream might become a reality. Bath is surrounded by villages which sound as if the builders had short-term memory loss: Bathampton, Bathford, Bathwick, and our first destination, Batheaston. We were due to meet Maxine, the estate agent, who would show us four houses pre-selected by us from details we received before departure.

The owners of the first house clearly loved dressing up, because every room contained fancy-dress clothes and what looked like props from period dramas. Maxine opened the door to the down-stairs bathroom with the kind of flourish that can only come from opening doors for years. We were greeted by a suggestive photo, which we all managed to make no reference to in spite of the fact that it covered the whole wall of a tiny room. The next house was a six-storey Georgian town house right in the centre of Bath. Tempting – but with tiny children completely impractical.

Saltford Manor was the third house on our list – back in London it had been our least favourite, a view which Maxine clearly shared. She did something which must rank as a first in the history of estate agency: she tried to put us off going. The facts were on her side: it was in bad repair and hundreds of other couples had seen it and were not impressed. We were behind schedule and there was every reason to skip this house and move on to the final one, which on paper looked much more attractive. I have many character faults which, after fifteen years of marriage, were all too obvious to Anna, but one of the most deep-seated is stubbornness. By now this was the only house I wanted to see. And so we drove west out of Bath, following the Avon valley to the ivy-covered gates announcing themselves in grand gold letters as Saltford Manor. This was a long way from our two-bedroom terrace in London. Maxine struggled with a huge set of rusty keys, clearly ordered from the props department of Hammer films. Finally the padlock fell away and we helped her push the old gates open. We left the girls asleep in their car seats, hacked our way through the shoulder-high undergrowth, jumped over the trench that had been dug immediately outside the front door and waited for Maxine to join us on the other side. She opened the door and we stepped inside.

Confident that it would not be long before we retreated, Maxine stayed firmly anchored to the front door; no time for opening doors and pointing out the generosity of the cupboard space here. The inside of the house was in worse repair than the outside. It had suffered two separate pipe bursts and two of the main rooms had no ceilings, which meant that two of the bedrooms had no floors. Walking in virtual silence through empty room after empty room, we were able to view three floors, twelve rooms, in less than five minutes. The top floor was a maze of water tanks and lead piping balanced precariously on beams and half hidden by straw-filled partitions: the fifties version of plasterboard. Clearly this was a house that defied all normal criteria. Downstairs, most of the rooms had walls which were in places four feet thick. Many of them were considerably thicker at the bottom than the top and there was nothing approaching a right angle in the place.

In the hall, the ceiling was supported by huge irregularly cut oak timbers, some of which were three foot square. At the top of the winding oak staircase, on the landing, there was a wall of beautiful mellowed oak panelling lit by a small three-light window, the kind you would expect to see in an ancient church. This was some place. I paused for breath and glanced again at the estate agents' details: 'In need of restoration', so far so true. 'Many fascinating period features' seemed to me even then to be a very restrained description of what I thought was a treasure chest of gems. In the bedroom the beams on the ceiling were more finely cut and set into carved cross-beams perhaps twelve feet above our heads. To the left stood a beautifully carved stone fireplace with the initials AF and LF and the date 1637 carved into the high lintel. I wondered a little about AF and LF. Had they slept in this room? Their initials were also to be seen above the mantelpiece downstairs but supplemented by 'EF' and the date 1645 – why? But nothing had prepared me for the bedroom's massive window, described by the agents as 'magnificent'. Never in the undistinguished history of estate agents' particulars has a word been used so appropriately. It consisted of two windows with rounded Norman arches, set within a recess that was framed by two finely carved columns with beautifully fluted heads and crowned with another, larger rounded arch that was decorated with intricate zigzag carving. I knew that I had never seen a window like this in any house I had ever been in. If we lived here we could get up, take in this 'magnificent' window, which the agent's details described as Norman, glance fleetingly at the seventeenth-century fireplace and while raising our eyes upwards in a gesture of thanksgiving take in the Tudor beams. Not bad for the day's first trip to the bathroom.

The country dream, however, is not primarily about architecturally interesting trips around a house; it is about an almost primal desire to be close to something that at least looks like nature. Five miles from an attractive place like Bath, this costs plenty of money. When we had begun searching for a house early in the summer we had a completely unrealistic idea of what our money would buy. There was a tension: we needed to stay reasonably close to London because of work, but we also wanted more space for our money and money wasn't something we had in great abundance. Anna had worked in publishing and I had been an actor and a BBC employee, neither likely to bring in big bucks. We had no aspirations to live in a big country house, and had never once talked of buying even a listed house, never mind one like this. We wanted a garden for the children to play in and perhaps a fourth bedroom. Yet here we were at the gates of Saltford Manor – a treasure trove of possibilities which went, confusingly, under the name of a house. At £5,000 less than we thought we might get for our two-bedroom terraced cottage in London, this place looked very reasonably priced.

Anyone who has walked around a house with a view to living there will know that something rather unusual happens in those moments. Like all potential purchasers we were trying to lift all the components of our lives and drop them down in front of this new and, at first sight, rather alarming backdrop. I knew at the deepest level that this was an astonishing place, full of the most remarkable features held together in what I thought was a delightfully haphazard fashion. But I also knew that the task of transforming this beautiful but tired heap of stone and timber into a house in which Anna and I and two pre-school children could live would be enormous.

The most pressing question was how much was this broken-down old place going to cost to put right? Back in London I got hold of the Bath Yellow Pages, thumbed up the sections headed 'Surveyors and Local Planning' (the house was listed Grade II*) and set up a meeting back at the house a week later. Simon the Surveyor was all deference and corduroy, Bob the Planner all enthusiasm and electric blue jeans. Surprisingly they made a happy combination.

Bob had made a study of old English architecture and spoke with a soft West Country accent. The Norman inhabitants would have lived in one huge room on the first floor. The animals would have sheltered downstairs and the access would have been up wooden stairs on the outside at the back of the building and through an opening onto what is now the top of the landing. The original opening is now filled with a small church-style window salvaged from what may well have been an Elizabethan chapel which collapsed just before the Second World War. Bob seemed to lose momentum and slumped onto the stairs visibly shaken. The blood drained from his face. He had been weakened by reminding himself that an Elizabethan chapel had been allowed to collapse. And then he spotted the small narrow tunnel which went from what he had just told us was the old front door to a space that we had intended to use as a linen cupboard. Back on his feet and speaking with the quiet authority of someone who really knew, Bob pronounced that this was probably a peephole to enable those inside the house to identify visitors who had climbed the external staircase. Security, it seemed, was just as much an issue for the Normans as it is for us. Simon spoke with passion about letting the building breathe and Bob spoke of morning sunlight falling on the mellow stone of the mullioned windows. They were off in a world of their own, floating happily between the twelfth and seventeenth centuries, and I wanted to join the party.

I reminded myself that we needed to leave with a cost estimate for renovation and tried to pull us back to earth by asking a sequence of dull, detailed questions about heating and plumbing. Simon and Bob were not for turning. My questions only succeeded in triggering a fascinating discourse about the insulation values of Elizabethan glass and the location of possible wells in the garden. They were talking poetry, I was talking overdraft. They could see I was nervous about taking on such a big project and somehow managed to give me the feeling that we were all in this together. 'Go on!' Bob said kindly. 'You love the place. Have a go.'

We had an anxious moment in the garden when the two men expressed different views about the church next door. Simon said that his parents, who lived in the village, liked the place but found it a bit too 'alleluia' for their tastes, whereas Bob's reservations were of a different nature. Some years ago the church had submitted an application to build a modern extension to the side because they were unable to seat everyone who wished to come to the popular Sunday-morning service. Feelings ran high in the village, meetings were called and views expressed, but eventually the application was rejected on the grounds of preserving the community's historical heritage. Notwithstanding his clear disbelief that the church was ever full, Bob could not understand how issues of seating could matter more than the shape of a historical building. The moment passed and we went to a pub, looked at the figures and returned to London thinking that financially at least it might just be possible.

The logistics of upping and leaving London were considerable. Where were we going to live while the work on the house was undertaken? How would we find the right builders to do the work? Could we trust them? What about the move itself? Should we go with Pickfords or Roger's Removals? But there was a much bigger question: did we really want to change everything and leave London? For years we had talked about it but now it was a reality. The senior estate agent – Maxine's boss – was considerably less relaxed than Maxine had been. Without knowing it we had entered the emotionally charged world of buying and selling houses in which even the slightest thing like the word 'woodworm' can trigger an anxious phone call:

'Is there any woodworm?'

'No. My clients have long guarantees.'

'How long?'

'Oh gosh – I am not entirely sure – I'll need to double-check with my colleague Dominic on this one. Are you around later on?'

'Yes. Could you call me when you know?'

'Sure.' (He puts his hand over the mouthpiece. I catch the phrase 'bombing over with the keys'.) 'Sorry, things are crazy here just now. In the last couple of weeks we've noticed the market hardening up – very exciting.'

'Yes very.' (Not for me though.) 'Well, can you find out?'

'Yes, yes of course.' (Pause.) 'About what?'

'The woodworm.'

'No problem.'

At the bottom of agents' particulars there is an understated warning that they cannot be relied upon as 'statements or representations of fact'. In other words there is just enough reality, like the photo on the front, to make the reader believe all is well. In our case all was far from well. We entered a fog of indecision. Before, discussions had been about why we needed to stay whereas now they were about why we needed to leave. Over the years we had become city dwellers; we loved the edgy excitement of London and the eclectic range of people in our lives. Suddenly it seemed much harder to leave. But time and estate agents wait for no man – certainly not one who might buy a house.

'Hello Mr Wynn – how are you?'

'Fine.'

'Good, good. Since we last spoke we've had considerable interest in Saltford and thought it only fair to come back to you.'

'Thank you.'

'My client is keen to progress matters and has suggested that we go for best and finals by Monday.'

'Right.'

'I said I would speak to you first just to see how you felt.'

'Slightly confused.'

'I know it is difficult – the press don't make it easy.'

(Now very worried – surely the press haven't heard about the house?) 'Pardon?'

'All the speculation about the American elections and the market going spongy. It's making local buyers nervous but not, thankfully, the city boys. There's always plenty of them.'

'I see.'

'Out here they get more bang for their bucks. We had a young guy in this morning.' (Noises off.) 'Excuse me Mr Wynn.' (He puts his hand over the mouthpiece – more mumbling followed by the phrase 'sealed bids tomorrow'.) 'Sorry Mr Wynn. It's gone mad again!'

'Yes. Well – thank you.'

'Not at all – in fairness I just wanted to keep you in the frame.'

Clearly we needed to reach a decision. That same week Anna drove down to Bath for the day and looked at our rental options. We would need to find somewhere to live for six months – possibly a year – whilst the house was being restored. She bought the local paper and made some calls, looked at a flat above the local sweetshop and a semi-detached farm cottage known to Simon the Surveyor on the edge of the village. Avon Cottage, Avon Lane – sounded very idyllic. I phoned the owner of the cottage to arrange a viewing. On arrival it turned out that a couple of large sheep dogs had been in residence and the carpets were thick with dog hairs, so I asked whether it would be possible for him to have the carpets cleaned before we moved in. There was a long pause. Surely this was a reasonable request or had I broken some mysterious country code? No, he replied, that would be fine but obviously it would depend on the weather. It was difficult to see quite where we could go from this point; we were not connecting, so I let the matter drop and moved on to safer subjects like money and dates.

I understood the necessity for sensible planning; the truth was that in my mind we had already moved into the most magical place I had ever seen. But Anna and I saw the situation very differently. I smelt history, she smelt drains; and there were plenty of them flowing in an authentic medieval way through the garden. With less than a week to go before we had to make a decision Anna remembered an evening over a year before when we had invited some friends for supper. Right at the end of an otherwise unremarkable evening, Richard, who happened to be an Anglican vicar, said that he had a strong sense that we would be connected with a place called St Mary's. The name St Mary's had meant nothing to us but Richard clarified his feeling by saying he felt that we would be a 'supporting wall for a place called St Mary's'. We thought nothing much of this information until Anna, who had been studying the drawing on the back of the agent's details, noticed that the 'adjacent church' to Saltford Manor was called St Mary's. The garden and the churchyard share the same wall.

We bundled the children into the car yet again and booked ourselves into a B & B on the edge of Bath. The next day was Sunday and we decided to attend the morning service at St Mary's to give us one final chance to check out the house. I do not know the correct way to approach going to church, but I do know that on that morning my way was not it. One thought had dominated my every waking moment for the last month and as I sat in that ancient place of worship, it screamed for attention: did the house next door have my name on it? I am no Bible expert but I knew enough to appreciate that when Jesus spoke about building a house upon a rock, this was not what he meant.

The service began harmlessly enough and then after five minutes someone stood up and read a passage from the Bible which began with the words: 'This is what the Lord Almighty says: reform your ways and your actions, and *I will let you live in this place.*' To say these words got my attention would be an understatement. It was as if a spotlight had picked me out, time stood still and I felt as if I was the only person there. The reading lasted no more than two minutes and finished with these words: 'if you do not follow other gods to your own harm, then *I will let you live in this place,* in the land I gave to your forefathers for ever and ever'. At the end of the service a lady approached me outside the church and with the house looming behind her told me that she had found herself praying for me during the service. She wondered if I had some issue on my mind?

The next day I rang Dominic and made an offer, which was accepted. We had crossed some invisible line and after months, even years, of dreaming about country life, had moved closer to waking up. In the real world of buying and selling houses I knew that my conversation with Dominic meant nothing at all. The place was not ours until we had the money and had exchanged contracts.

Buying any house in England is, as everyone knows, one of life's most stressful events, but buying an old house is even worse. Within a week the bank manager was on the phone alarmed by the word 'uninhabitable' which had appeared in his surveyor's report. He maintained that the word meant no one could live in the place and therefore he was unable to authorise a loan. I tried over a period of some days to arrive at a broader definition of the word but he was not impressed. If ever there was a defining moment this was it. Now that we were so close to losing it I realised how much I wanted it and went into hyperdrive. I reached, once again, for the Yellow Pages and found an independent local surveyor known to the bank. I asked for a report to persuade an unimaginative bank manager that in spite of the collapsed ceilings, lack of floors and holes in the roof, the place was really a contemporary lifestyle statement. It must have been one of the shortest surveys ever written, containing as it did the words 'gas', 'water', 'electricity' and very little else. Amazingly, it worked. The bank agreed to lend the money.

A couple of weeks before moving, Sebastian, the man from the removal firm, arrived on our doorstep. He was tall, with long floppy fair hair, which he was constantly sweeping back. He told us that he had been out on the vans and apologised about his clothes: faded but expensive jeans, dusty suede loafers and tailored blue shirt with slightly frayed collar and cuffs. I instantly felt very underdressed. He strode around our small house logging the contents in one of those old-fashioned notebooks that solicitors and barristers use. He had more in common with an Oxford postgraduate than most of the removal men I had met, but no matter. The price was fair and he seemed to know what he was doing. He was going to come back and do the job with one of his colleagues, Piers. And then, with one final flick of his beautifully cut hair, he was gone.

We were both blinking back the tears as we limped silently onto the Westway. In the space of the two-hour journey to Bath I swung from elation to despair and back – five times. I felt responsible – the excitement about the house had been almost all mine and I was worried that I had been selfish and was dragging Anna and the girls away from a place they knew and loved to go somewhere which might be a disaster. We arrived at Avon Cottage to find the owner putting the finishing touches to a carpet display in the garden. The weather was fine and so, true to his word, he had assembled the carpets on the washing lines in readiness for the cleaning we had requested. He said that beating the carpets should only take a couple of minutes but that he needed a couple more hours to squeeze what he called 'the last few bits', but which looked to us to be the entire contents of his house, into the garage. I left Anna filling plastic bin liners with empty cans of Fosters and drove into Bath to the estate agents to pick up the keys to Saltford Manor. I think I had in mind a 'significant' moment – if not exactly a ceremony then at least the keys laid out and ready, perhaps in an envelope with my name on. When I arrived I thought the place was empty until I looked again and saw someone skulking around in the shadows.

'Hi – I'm Dominic. Can I help you?'

He sounded and looked chillingly like Sebastian. Was he related?

'I've come to pick up the keys.'

'Great – which keys?'

'Saltford Manor.'

'Oh sorry – *you're* Mr Wynn.'

I shared his disappointment. He disappeared back to the shadows and rattled around inside a wall cupboard.

'Sorry, they're out.'

'They can't be – I bought the place today.'

'There's obviously been a bit of a balls-up – 'scuse my French.' More scurrying. 'Oh wait a mo, here they are.'

That was it. No ceremony, no electricity – just a rusty bunch of keys identified by a torn parcel label marked 'altford keys'. And yet in spite of this they looked good.

'Thank you,' I said, 'it's a great place.'

'It will be,' he said, pausing just long enough to make me nervous, 'one day.'

I was on the pavement before the penny finally dropped – the set of *Four Weddings and a Funeral*. That was where Sebastian, Piers and Dominic must have met. I put the keys on the passenger seat next to me and drove back to Saltford with the streets of Bath framed, like the opening title sequence to a movie. London was only a hundred miles away but as the pictures dissolved one into another it seemed like another country.

# · 2 ·

# Another Country

EARLY THE FOLLOWING evening, in the dapple-soft autumn light, I visited the house alone. Like a man in a dream, I approached the gates, no longer intimidating but charming. The drive, bedecked with wild flowers that fell freely from every crevice, pulled up a gentle incline before curving up to the left. It had been cleverly landscaped to keep the house hidden from the outside world. To my right stood a wild, strangely shaped copper beech tree, behind which was a tangle of overgrown shrubs and trees hiding what must once have been a meandering path. Weeds in wheel shapes shot long spindles of green which spiralled out of control. Further up the drive was a high curved wall, topped with mottled coping stones and almost completely hidden behind a tangle of rambling roses and shrubs which originated in the church-yard beyond. This wall started low just inside the gates and grew in height, curving round until it reached a small door which had, once upon a time, opened into the churchyard. Next to this and on our side of the wall stood a wood shed, whose back wall had been built around a substantial yew tree. I glided, as dreamers do, over a thatch of weeds and wild grass to the far corner of the garden to see the whole picture. Beyond the high wall and dwarfing the church were three glorious Scots pines, deep green branches arching high above the ground. Set against the clear evening sky, they reminded me of trees I had seen close to the sea. On this, my first unaccompanied visit to what was now our house, I knew I had found a place to stay, a place for children to grow up.

The main body of the house stood three storeys high, nine mullioned windows spread across its face, with a two-storey addition running out in the direction of the church.

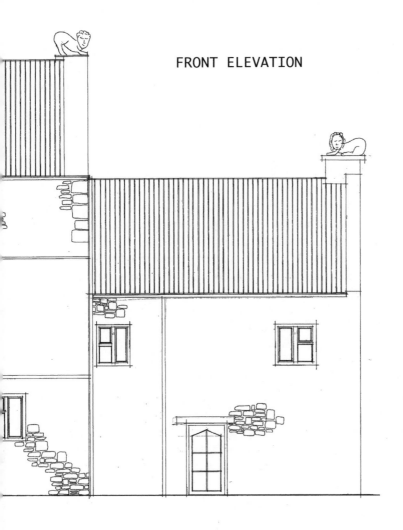

FRONT ELEVATION

Both sections were topped by ochre-red clay tiles. Its face was in the grip of ivy whose bony knuckles had entirely covered two windows, fingers forcing open the frames, as if trying to strangle the place. From where I stood the house looked as if it had lost hope. Dirty torn curtains hung limply inside the windows and an unconvincing sign alerting trespassers to 'Beware of the Dog' lay propped against the wall. But as I opened the front door, leaving it ajar to let the light fall inwards, it seemed to me that this house had not given up, that it was merely pausing, waiting to be revived. I went from room to room, as if for the first time.

The front door opened directly onto the hall, with a simple Norman stone arch and massive beams chaotically placed overhead. I tried to work out the logic of this arrangement but there was none and that, I remembered, was the joy of the place. Everywhere I looked there were slopes, curves and angles. Two main downstairs rooms led directly off the hall: to the right the dining room, to the left the drawing room. In the latter, a burst pipe had caused the ceiling to collapse; it was now a room with a broken back. The fireplace, covered in a thick blanket of dust, was undamaged and quite beautiful. A substantial but delicate oak mantelpiece complete with a row of small carved arches, like a run of miniature church windows, was held up by two finely carved stone columns. Even the dirty beige gloss paint which covered them could not disguise their beauty. The people who made this fireplace were more than craftsmen, they must have been artists. Above the fireplace was a finely cast piece of plasterwork, containing shields and emblems, like those I had seen in National Trust houses. In the centre of the plasterwork, which spanned the whole width of the fireplace and reached up to what was left of the high ceiling cornicing, was the date 1645 – which I remembered from school history marked the end of the English Civil War. To the left of the fireplace was a large bookcase, hanging like a partially open door, behind which was a sizeable empty space. What had this mysterious space been used for? In between two large mullioned windows with high window seats cut into the massively thick walls was a large wedge-shaped stone supporting the ceiling. Bob the Planner had said that it was part of the original Norman structure. I loved its rough creamy simplicity.

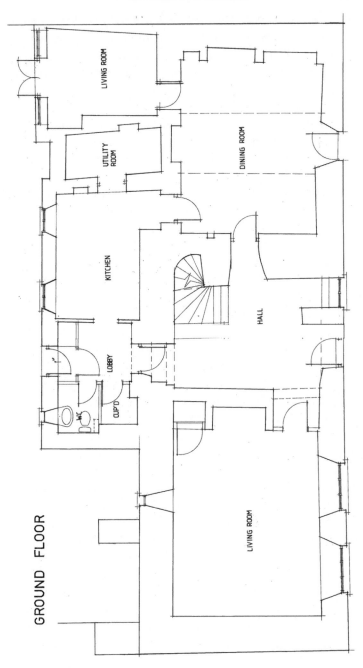

GROUND FLOOR

LIVING ROOM

UTILITY ROOM

DINING ROOM

KITCHEN

HALL

LOBBY

WC

CUP'D

LIVING ROOM

Back through the hall, I was now in a relatively modern extension at the back of the house which looked onto the back garden and rolling fields beyond. Through what had clearly been a kitchen and through another ancient old door into the other main room downstairs, I found myself in what had been the dining room. This room could also be accessed from the hall. The ceiling here was lower than the drawing room, with wooden beams more classically arranged than the chaos of the hall. There was a large old farmhouse-type fireplace, which would make a wonderful enclave for a wood-burning stove. With some work and loads of imagination this would make a great family kitchen. This room led to another small room, part of the single-storey extension, which also looked onto the fields.

The stairs led off the hall, and curved upwards and round a corner. I recalled from our first visit that this had been one of the joys of the place. The house was a series of surprises, each corner revealing some unexpected sight. At the top of the stairs, up another three steps and standing on my left was a wall of mellow oak panelling. Opposite was an oak cupboard under the stairs up to the second floor. Behind the oak wall was the smallest bedroom (bedroom 3), in which was a pretty window seat looking onto the front garden and a mysterious blanked-off window, whose sides were framed by a pair of wall paintings. On one side were depicted the Virgin and Child and on the other a man with curly hair holding a circle over his heart. The images had the two-dimensional simplicity of children's paintings and I had a dim recollection of seeing figures like these in books about art history and in frescoes in Italian churches, but certainly never in any house that I had ever been in. I felt, just for that moment, that I was seeing into the very life of things, seeing something I had never seen before, as if I had been allowed to look with an eye made quiet at something almost sacred.

Next door was the master bedroom with the 'magnificent' window and the high stone fireplace dated 1637 and inscribed with the initials AF and LF. What had happened in 1637 and where was EF? This had been the room which had entranced me most on our first visit. The window had been carved out of blocks of pink stone and was essentially two high narrow panes of glass, crowned with a double-grooved hood, supported by half-shafts whose tops were engraved with fluted

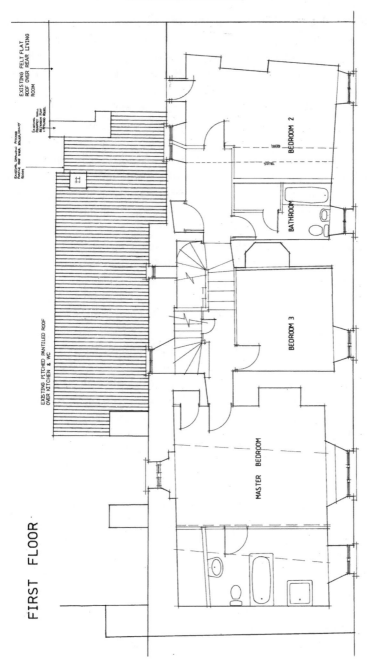

FIRST FLOOR ·

EXISTING FELT FLAT ROOF OVER REAR LIVING ROOM

EXISTING PITCHED PANTILED ROOF OVER KITCHEN & WC

BEDROOM 2

BATHROOM

BEDROOM 3

MASTER BEDROOM

scallops. This shape was set within two larger matching frames, like a picture within a picture within a picture, all three of which were crowned by an arch decorated with finely cut lozenge shapes. Like the paintings next door, it was a feature I associated with a castle or a church but not a house. But, and this was its charm, it managed to be both majestic and awe-inspiring without being intimidating. Its majesty lay in its size – the ledge at the bottom was large enough to seat three grown men – and in another quality more difficult to define. The men who created this window had thought big thoughts. As I looked out through its diminishing soft pink frames, nothing seemed quite normal. Soaked in serenity as these stones were, they seemed to hold a promise for the future. I tried in vain to imagine us all living here. The place felt unreal – not least the bathroom. It was huge; huge, that is, compared to our cramped one in London, and was complete with one of those cast-iron baths which stand on two pairs of animal claws.

Retracing my way along the first-floor landing, I saw another bathroom to the right and a short lower landing leading into another bedroom (bedroom 2), over what I had imagined would become the kitchen. The ceiling had partially collapsed, but rather than making the room seem broken in this case it seemed to be an improvement. In the open space above the old false ceiling stood the huge oak A-frames, some of which were covered in bark, which held the roof up. In this upper section was a water tank and pipes, which had burst.

I walked back along the landing and on up the final flight of stairs to the top of the three-storey part of the house.

On my left was a small unremarkable room (bedroom 5), and ahead an ancient-looking wooden door so twisted that I looked twice. The door led to a mess of damp plasterboard hiding another tangle of tanks and burst pipes (bedroom 4). This was potentially the best room of all because it was very large, with windows on three sides. The floor had been eccentrically inserted at a level which allowed the crest of the Norman window to peep up from the bedroom below. Above I saw more wooden A-frames supporting this section of the roof. This room sat at the top of the house, high above the world.

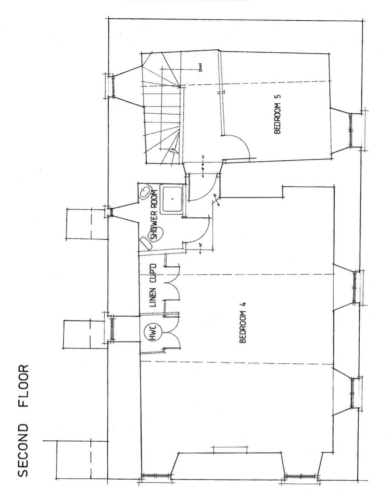

SECOND FLOOR

BEDROOM 5

BEDROOM 4

SHOWER ROOM

LINEN CUPD

HWC

The evening was warm and amber as I wandered into the wilderness of the back garden; a sort of Eden, a world so quiet it seemed unreal. Looking out over the fields to the gently rising hills beyond, I did not see how we could ever tire of living here. The wall separating the garden from the church had shrunk to waist height, now offering only a token partition. I sat on it, soaked up the last few moments of sun and took in the rear elevation: half house, half church. This was a place to fold the hands and rest.

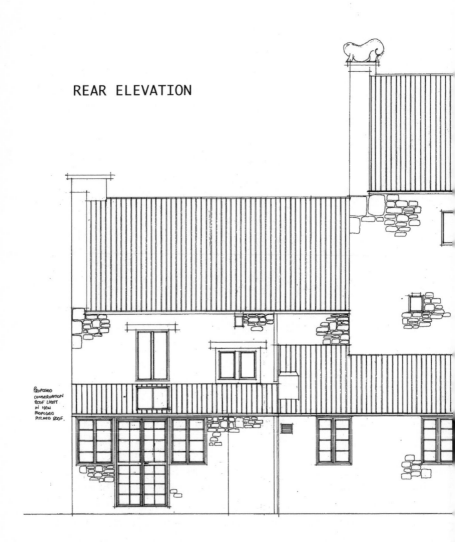

REAR ELEVATION

PROPOSED
CONSERVATION
ROOF LIGHT
IN NEW
PROPOSED
PITCHED ROOF.

'Hi.'

I turned to see a bearded figure clad in jeans and trainers, striding purposefully towards me. At first sight he looked like the man who had been taking the service on our earlier visit on that fateful Sunday, but then he had been wearing a dog collar and robes. I was cautious. Nothing had been normal this evening and so, still not sure who he was, I settled for something safe.

'Hi.'

'How are you doing?'

Yes, it was Chris the Curate, I remembered his voice.

'It's my turn to look after the Climbers,' he said cheerfully.

What was he saying? When I had last seen him he had been introducing hymns, now he was doubling as a gardener. But evening light can play strange tricks and I thought that perhaps, like many people in dreams, Chris had taken on a different identity. And then, quite suddenly, something very real happened. A group of teenagers, all rucksacks and laces, appeared on the path – and punctured the bubble of my dream.

'We're putting on a Sunday-school play.' He gestured to the teenagers, who were, it transpired, part of what he called a Climbers group.

'Great.'

'I was actually going to ask you if you would like to lend a hand. Someone told me you used to be an actor and I thought it might be your sort of thing . . .'

This was no longer a dream, or even a possible dream, this had now become a nightmare. It was true that ages ago I had been an actor, but although it had been fun at the time I had stopped because I did not think I was cut out for it. I had earned a living for ten years by being in plays and did not want to be in any play ever again – and certainly not in this place where we were trying to build a new life. But before it was necessary to say anything, there was a loud shriek and he disappeared inside the church to do some pruning.

In the weeks that followed, I discovered that in relation to ancient buildings like the church or this house, the village felt a sense of corporate ownership. One Sunday morning Brian, whose wife Joyce did the church flowers, asked me if I would show him around the house. Brian had recently retired from the merchant navy and he and Joyce had moved to Saltford to be near their grandchildren. Eventually we arrived at the large room at the top of the house, so high it probably reminded him of being on the bridge of a ship. He fiddled with the leather buttons on his cardigan.

'James?' He was speaking confidentially, as I imagined he might to a fellow officer. 'I don't quite know how to say this . . .'

'If it's anything I've done . . .'

'No, no, please. What . . . what I'm getting at . . .' And then, quite suddenly, he pulled himself up to his full height and it all came out in a rush.

'I think we all owe you a great vote of thanks.'

'Sorry?'

'For all this.' He gestured around the room.

'I'm not with you.'

'If you had not come along this place would have fallen down and we would all have been the losers.'

'I don't see it like that.'

'I know, that's why I want you to know how we all feel.' Brian had rather crumpled and was addressing his buttons, which he was now undoing. 'Sorry, I'm not very good at this sort of thing . . . speeches and all that.'

I was really touched. I had thought that we might be seen as hostile intruders but in fact the very opposite appeared to be the case. The village was sad to see the house falling into disrepair and glad that someone was prepared to take it on and love it back to life.

In the first few weeks there was so much to do: boxes to unpack, children to be settled in, not to mention the small task of restoring a house. I began to visit the public library on my way to the builders' merchants, curious to find out more about the place. After a couple of snatched visits it became clear I had unwittingly joined a collection of people engaged in similar work. I found myself staring wistfully at the shelves stacked with videos and DVDs, which suddenly became very attractive.

It's in the pages of the Anglo-Saxon Chronicle that the name Saltford makes its first appearance. In AD 520 a native warlord, thought by some to have been the legendary King Arthur, crossed the River Avon at a place then known as 'Sahl-ford', meaning 'ford with trees', in pursuit of the waves of invading Saxons who came from what we now call Denmark into Southampton waters in the early part of the sixth century. The historical status of King Arthur is still hotly debated. But if such a figure did exist it seems likely that he was a native warlord leading the resistance to the Saxon invaders. Certainly, his associations with the West Country are strong; Cadbury Castle, which rises abruptly out of the gentle Somerset countryside some sixty miles south of 'Sahl-ford', is often identified as one of his strongholds, and in the 1950s fragments of sixth-century pottery similar to those found at Tintagel in Cornwall – where Arthur is supposed to have been born – were discovered there. There was also the outline of a great feasting hall, thought to date from the same period. Excavations suggested that the community which occupied this ancient hill fort during these years was colossal, upwards of 1,000 armed men and their families, all protected by a drystone wall which ran around the entire 18-acre enclosure.

It would have taken Arthur and his rough band of Celtic horsemen perhaps two days to reach the river crossing at 'Sahl-ford'. Had they paused at the top of the hill overlooking the river they would have seen swathes of lime-green willow branches brushing lightly across the sleepy water. At the bottom of the hill, which fell gently away towards the river, were the huts and enclosures of a small farming community. The fields spreading out as far as the eye could see were easy to work; the river was tidal (river locks were over a thousand years away), which made the brown soil soft and rich and the crops plentiful. The meander in the river, framed by willows and fertile meadows, would have been a good place for an overnight camp, protected as it was by the river and the hill. Or perhaps they just waited a few hours for the low tide before lifting their shields and javelins overhead and leading their horses chest-high through the water in pursuit of the invading Saxons. The Welsh monk Nennius wrote that the Saxons were crushed 'with great slaughter . . . nine hundred and sixty men fell in a single onslaught'. But the effect of Arthur's victory on the future of England was short-lived. Within a generation the Saxons and another tribe of invaders called the Angles had created a culture in lowland Britain, which they called England – 'Angle-land'.

Today the house overlooks the stretch of water once called 'ford with trees' but now known, rather less poetically, as the Shallows. At the bottom of the hill, some two minutes' walk from the house, there is a row of cottages set back from the river as it wanders through meadows many of which are still fringed with willow trees. Mike, whom I had decided to ask to do the general building work, lived in one of these cottages. He had recently completed work on the village hall and came highly recommended. It proved to be a good decision. He hired a couple of muscular Australian students, from the Backpackers Hostel in Bath, and set to work. They hacked off old plaster, removed the half-inch of cement that lay between the earth and our feet, and dug out the whole of the ground floor. Two weeks after they had started, the house looked naked.

The first weeks of preparatory building work continued to bring new clues to light. On the ground floor, through the Norman arch, was a pantry which we wanted to convert into a coat cupboard. In the course of stripping back the walls of this space, ready for new plaster, we found a rusty iron shape about the length of a hand, which finished in a sharp point. Sitting on piles of cement bags in front of the fifteenth-century oak mantelpiece, the four of us had coffee and passed our 'treasure' around. The Australians, who were fascinated by any finds predating 1950, decided that it must be an arrowhead from the Battle of Hastings. Mike went for something closer to home – a kitchen fork. And then, more remarkably, beneath the upstairs floorboards we discovered a tiny room below, sealed on one side by the pantry and on the other by the back of the bookcase in the lounge. This must have been what the books called a priest's hole, a cell where priests could hide. This meant that the family living in the house during the sixteenth century was probably Catholic.

Having stripped back the house internally, Mike mentioned, casually late one afternoon, that we needed a new wide-gauge water pipe from the mains supply outside the gates to the house. We were waiting for the water board to provide us with the exact location of the mains, the builders' merchants were out of wide-gauge pipe, and Simon the Surveyor was on holiday. It was therefore surprising, and not a little alarming, to arrive the next morning to find Mike sat astride a digger, like a tank commander, tearing up huge chunks of rock in preparation for a new water pipe. Within two days there was a channel, deep enough to hide a standing man, which started at the front gates and cut diagonally across the garden finishing at the threshold of the front door. To Mike it was just another trench, to me it looked like a wound, but to the Australians, who were now convinced that the arrowhead was from William the Conqueror's own bow, it was an opportunity for more archaeological discovery.

I explained that others had been here before us and showed them, by way of proof, a faded newspaper article, published in 1913, which mentioned the recent discovery in the cellar of a sword thought to date from the sixteenth century. The reference to a cellar was puzzling because the ground floor had been stripped back to the earth and there was no sign of an entrance. Nevertheless, for centuries people had talked, as they continue to do, about an underground passage from the house to the church next door and even to Keynsham Abbey some three miles away. Was there some long-established connection between Keynsham and Saltford? Certainly Keynsham had Saxon roots. In 871 the Bishop of Sherbourne was killed during one of the Viking raids and his body was brought to 'Caegineshame' for burial. The shaft of a Saxon cross has been found built into the foundations of the abbey and, a more recent discovery, a grave slab, book clasp and strap have also been found. Perhaps the entrance to the passage, if it existed at all, started under the concrete floor of the garage where our furniture was now stored. But whether or not such a passage existed, many people continued to think that it did; as if something in the community memory bank just 'knew' Saltford and Keynsham were linked.

In those early months, there was so much that was new, so much to learn. In this part of the country many people use 'he' or 'she' to describe inanimate objects. Tools, bag of cement, even underground passages become personalised. One Sunday morning I saw two men with dogs on their way up the path to the fields beyond the house. They stopped outside the gates and stared at the freshly dug trench, which provided new material for the ongoing debate about the reality of the secret underground passage to Keynsham.

'Perhaps they found him?'

'Don't be daft. He'd be for the internet.'

'No – he's too big. He goes *to* Keynsham mind, not away from it.'

'That's why he's so clever.'

'Why's that then?'

'He's a decoy – they know what they was about in them days.'

Underground passages, priest's holes and Elizabethan chapels – there were so many questions and so few answers. I returned to the library keener than ever and was delighted to find that in 1086 Saltford Manor appeared in the nearest thing the Normans had to estate agents' details – the Domesday Book. The entry for Saltford reads as follows:

> The land of the Bishop of Coutances, Roger Witten, holds of the Bishop – Saltford. Four thegns held in parage. T.R.E and paid geld for 4 hides. There is land for 6 ploughs. In demesne there for 7 hides, 3 ploughs and 6 serfs and there are 7 villeins and 10 borders with 4 ploughs and 2 hides. There are 1 riding horse, 13 swine and 120 sheep. There is a small mill paying twelve shillings and six pence, and thirty-two acres of meadow.

But like estate agents' details, old documents need decoding. Who was the Bishop of Coutances? He was called Geoffrey and he was chaplain-in-chief to the Norman forces at the Battle of Hastings. He brought a group of monks with him whose task it was to fight with their prayers. It was said of him that 'He knew better how to teach knights in their hauberks [mail armour] to fight than clerks in their vestments to sing psalms.' He spent the eve of the battle going around the camp hearing confessions in a 'religious frenzy'.

Christmas Day 1066 found Bishop Geoffrey next to William the Conqueror, Duke of Normandy, at his coronation in the abbey of Westminster. The circumstances of 1066, the death of the English King Harold at Hastings and the subsequent coronation of a Norman monarch, demanded new protocol. Geoffrey, speaking in French, and Aldred, Archbishop of York, speaking in English, asked the congregation whether they would accept the new King – an innovation imported from France and one which is still a part of English coronations. The mercenary troops guarding the chapel misunderstood the shouts accompanying this new interactive bilingual ceremony, thought a riot was starting and began to set fire to the neighbouring houses as a diversion. Nothing, however, could stop the legal consequences of what had taken place. Duke William of Normandy was now King of England and the first registered owner of Saltford was at his side.

The next twenty years brought rebellion, hunger and disease as rebel English armies were battered into submission by the Normans, who plundered and raped, flattening crops and buildings as part of a systematic campaign to repress all resistance to Norman rule. King William spent Christmas 1085 at Gloucester, where, so the Anglo-Saxon Chronicle says, he had 'very deep discussion with his council about this country – how it was settled, and with what kind of people'. This was a polite way of saying he wanted to calculate the taxable capacity of the land he had conquered, now nearly twenty years earlier. The Chronicle continued, 'So very strictly did he have it investigated that there was no single hide nor yard of land, nor indeed (shame it is to relate but it seemed no shame to him to do) one ox nor one cow nor one pig was left out.' The survey, originally called the King's Book, soon became known as the Domesday Book, because it seemed to contain a record, like that to be revealed on Judgement Day, against which there could be no appeal. Seven groups of commissioners, under the authority of Bishop Geoffrey, travelled the length and breadth of the country to find out the value of landholdings and noted, amongst other things, that Saltford, probably at this stage a low wooden structure, had '13 swine and 1 riding horse'.

In 1086 most of the population lived in small villages. All but the five largest towns had less than a thousand inhabitants and places where large towns were later to be built, like Newcastle and Liverpool, were not yet even villages. For the people of Saltford life would have revolved around the manor and church at the top of the hill, and the mill, bakery and blacksmith clustered around the ford at the bottom. The mill was one of 5,624 listed in the Domesday Book, which calls it 'small'. That meant it was one of the recently constructed horizontal structures, probably built of oak with internal gear wheels of elm, to be found in almost every village across the land. It turned slowly but surely as day followed day, season followed season, pushed by the sleepy river water. The villagers, the borders, villeins and serfs mentioned in Domesday, lived in wooden huts made of sturdy beams through which were laced branches from the nearby willows. The whole structure was covered in a mix of clay, straw and cow dung. The roofs were covered with thatch and into the walls were cut narrow gaps, covered with wattle shutters.

Saltford was a small community, a total of 24 men and their families. Everyone was known – no need for surnames. The only man in the village who had a surname was Roger Witten, the man named in the first line of the Domesday entry. His surname, like the name of the village over which he had power, was Anglo-Saxon and meant 'the wise one'. Saltford's Domesday entry begins, 'The land of the Bishop of Countances, Roger Witten, holds of the Bishop – Saltford.' A clearer picture was emerging. Bishop Geoffrey, part of a small circle of Frenchmen given nearly a quarter of the land in England, had been granted over 280 English manors, one of which was Saltford.

Having completed a wholesale redistribution of the conquered territory, the Normans adapted the system of landholding known as feudalism, already developed during Anglo-Saxon times, to fit their military needs. It was based on one simple principle, services given in return for land held. After 1066 every square inch of England belonged to William, and his tenants-in-chief, like Bishop Geoffrey, had to pay for the privilege with 'service', which could mean grain, baskets of eggs, bacon, money or the supplying of knights and armed soldiers from the manors when the King wanted to go to war. The great men, like Bishop Geoffrey, could not possibly supervise all their lands and so sublet to men like Roger Witten, who in turn sublet to the men who worked the fields, Saltford's '7 villeins and 10 borders' and right at the bottom of the heap, '6 serfs'.

Behind these words lay a brutal fact: six men and their families, one quarter of Saltford's population, were slaves. This ratio almost perfectly reflects the proportion found across the region. Domesday records that most of the country's 28,285 slaves were to be found in the south and south-west. This was, in part, because Bristol was a slave port, trading with the merchants in Dublin, who ran what was the largest slave market in Western Europe. But it's perfectly possible that some of the Saltford Six were not products of Bristol's roaring trade in human flesh but had grown up in the village, choosing to make themselves the lord's property because they could no longer provide for their families. Famine was always just around the corner. There is an account, from an earlier time, of a village in Sussex which chose to commit suicide by jumping together from a nearby clifftop rather than face the slow and certain agony of starvation. In 1086 the starving man had no other resort than to kneel before his lord and place his head in his hands. 'Lord' derives from an Old English word meaning 'loaf-giver', suggesting that this route into slavery was common. But none of the men who worked the land were free in the sense that we understand the word. They could only gain their freedom by paying for it, a near-impossibility, or by running away, the price for which was death. To the 24 men listed in Domesday, whose families had looked out over the same gentle meander of water for as long as they, or anyone else, could remember, Bishop Geoffrey was a land-grabbing foreigner.

But decoding Domesday was a diversion from the main task, which was to get the house into a state in which we could live in it. The pressing need right now was for a cheap electrician. I had spent the first ten years of my working life hanging around studios and sets, waiting to say one line in a shot that was so wide no one would recognise me. I never became very good at acting but I did learn to appreciate the difference lighting could make to the mood of a scene. I began thinking of Saltford Manor, stripped back as it now was to the bare stone, as a film set. The scale plans which I had begun to prepare, against which I was asking builders to quote, looked more like shooting scripts than building plans. I started to read books which talked about lighting recipes, listing fittings called 'polestars' and 'echo wallwashes'. I walked around the house at different times of day and noted on my plans how the movement of the sun changed the light in each room. It was, I suppose, like going to a restaurant again and again and walking around the tables with a menu but never actually sitting down to eat. Eventually, the great day arrived; I met the first potential electrician. Armed with my increasingly complicated lighting plans we walked slowly around the house and I pointed out the position in the earth where I wanted four floor lights to backlight the arch in the hall. He listened patiently with that look of studied tolerance I had learnt to recognise and then, breaking with all normal practice, suddenly became personal.

'What a place – my girlfriend would just love this.'

That was it, I was off. William the Conqueror and Bishop Geoffrey, AF and LF, 1645; it all came tumbling out. I liked this man and felt that he must be the one to do the lights. He seemed to *understand* the place. And then he said something else, even more revealing.

'I don't know how you've made your money.'

I could see his point. My last job had been producing an audio-tape for a charity called Cats Protection which featured a cast of different cats miaowing – some sadly, some gratefully – which was going to be played whilst the receptionist put the caller on hold. It was not Hollywood and neither was the money. We were able to buy this place because some twenty-five years earlier I had landed a part in a television series which had enabled me to buy a small derelict flat in one of the cheaper parts of London. The flat cost me £7,150. In the mornings I rehearsed and in the afternoons I went back to my new home, dusted off the Black & Decker Workmate and got down to some carpentry, which over the years I grew to love. Five years later this flat was followed by another which in turn was followed by a small terraced house, all of which had needed extensive work. A pattern had been established: I worked as an actor when I could and filled in the gaps doing up flats and houses which meant that now we were, extraordinarily, able to exchange a two-up-and-two-down Victorian terraced cottage for the tumble-down wreck that Saltford Manor had become.

The previous owner had engaged a team of historical building consultants fresh from working on the fire-ravaged Windsor Castle to advise on how to make good the water damage caused by burst pipes. Their exhaustive reports were baffling and intimidating, full of jargon. This restoration business was clearly, if the consultants were to be believed, highly specialised work, not something for a small-time actor who had put up the odd shelf. And yet . . . I intu-itively knew what the house did *not* need was some 'treatment', which screamed design. The job, as I was beginning to see it, was to provide a simple frame through which the beauty of the place could be seen.

To walk through the front door was to step down half a metre and stand on packed earth that had not been moved for eight hun-dred years – not difficult to imagine Roger Witten standing in the same spot greeting the Domesday commissioners in the wet sum-mer of 1086. In the quiet of evening, with the house empty of builders and stripped of cables, lights, plaster and pipes, I stood in the hall on the bare earth and looked around. I saw raw stone and massive roof timbers and realised I was about to join the long line of people who had restored this house before me. Their images were inevitably blurred and incorrectly exposed, taken as they were by an amateur using a crude timer delay gauged in fractions of a millennium, and yet for all their imperfections they were becoming increasingly real to me. Sitting on the bottom step of the winding oak staircase, I ran my fingertips across the bare earth. A moment later I looked at my watch and an hour had passed. Peace: there was, after all, plenty of time.

Perhaps there was something sacred about the soil on which the first stones were laid, or perhaps it was some quality left by the people who had begun to wander through my imagination. Interestingly one of the questions we were often asked before leaving London was, does the house have a ghost? Three months into the building work my answer was – yes, it does. He is called the Holy Ghost and I want him to stay. A friend who I took through the house got close to describing the magnetism of the place. He paused in the large room at the top, the one I had always thought the most astonishing, and with damp eyes searched for words. 'I think it's the love, I can just feel it.' Tears often come when words stop and are always more articulate. They speak a language of worship and awe. This has always been a holy place.

# 3

# William's Window

F OR THE FIRST nine months of our time in Saltford we did not live at the Manor but in the cottage about half a mile away, over the fields at the back. Within a few weeks the first flush of adventure faded to be replaced by the reality of living in a small, cold, damp, broken-down, mice-friendly cottage, in the middle of fields. The owner had said the place was unique. He was right. You could take the floor tiles off the kitchen floor and stack them up in little piles, which was something most of the children who visited took great delight in doing. The bathroom, which was situated in a hastily constructed lean-to at the back of the property, had its own particular charms. The side of the bath would fall off when anyone opened or closed the door. It was the kind of feature a designer might build into a penthouse apartment. You know the sort of thing: the opening door activates the ISDN line, the side of the bath slides away to reveal a drop-down glass stairway leading to a backlit plunge pool. In our case the Blu-Tack® fell off, the stained MDF panel slumped forward and the colony of mice ran freely into the kitchen and beyond. Avon Cottage, which had seemed charming in September, was wretched in January.

Back in London we had talked of going on long rambling walks, pausing every now and then to look at wild flowers in the hedgerows. The reality was so very different. First, the climate seemed to have changed in the hundred miles between London and Bath. Every day brought rain, and more rain. Country walks, muddy at the best of times, were impossible with a buggy. But really there was no need to go out to study nature, it came to us. Wildlife in the shape of beetles, cockroaches, mice, woodlice and squirrels mounted an offensive on Avon Cottage. I cannot recall watching a television programme without a mouse, perhaps two, scuttling across the floor. Squirrels and pigeons took advantage of the tiles that were constantly blowing off the roof to shelter in the attic just above our bed. Our most frequent visitors were a couple of nice guys from A4 Pest Control. It was not very comforting to think they had chosen to name their company after *the* trunk road in the South-West of England; clearly they were busy. And then there were the nights. Country dark is different from city dark. The cottage was up an isolated lane a mile from the nearest house and Anna, on the few nights she was alone with the children, wanted to be somewhere else. The country dream, so long cherished, was falling to bits around us.

One evening we were about to eat supper, chicken and pasta as I recall, when there was a knock on the back door. A moment later, Anna came into the front room where I was sitting.

'There's someone to see you.'

'Who?'

She shrugged. 'Seems to know you – looks like a farmer.'

I glanced out of the window on my way through the kitchen, to see the back of a tall fair-haired man dressed in a cloth cap, a weathered Barbour jacket and muddy green boots. I arrived at the open door and he turned.

'Evening James.' It was Steve the electrician, who had, as it turned out, been at school with Mike.

'Steve, sorry I didn't recognise you.'

'I was just givin' the dogs a stretch. Gun dogs – don't like being inside.' I was surprised to find myself stroking the one closest to me. 'Said I'd pop over.'

I felt guilty for thinking he would forget. 'Thanks.'

'There's something I wanted to sort.'

He seemed as keen as me to find a date to start. Perhaps better not to pull out my diary, it might look a bit neurotic.

'You know all that old stone you got up at the Manor?'

'Mmm.'

'I just wondered if I could have a bit?'

'Sorry?'

'For my ponds.'

'Steve – you've lost me.'

'Them old fish ponds in the back field. I got a lease to look after them off the Parish Council.'

'Why?'

'I just thought it'd be great to take care of the place where the monks used to keep their fish.' The assumption that the ponds had once belonged to monks thought to have been living at the Manor had been a long and unchallenged part of village lore. 'To be honest with you, James, they're a bit broken down and I thought it'd be nice to use some of the stone up at the Manor. It seemed right somehow, what with the monks livin' there and all.'

'Absolutely – couldn't agree more.'

'OK – look, I'll pop round early tomorrow morning and load up a few.'

'Just a minute – I think it's a great idea but I really can't say we're not going to need them ourselves. There's masses still to do.'

'Fine – just thought I'd ask.' He paused and then almost as an afterthought: 'Actually there was one other thing.'

'Yes?'

'I wondered if I might bring my old parents up to look around – they're only round the corner in Norman Road. It'd be no problem for them.'

'Yes, of course.'

'My old mum used to work up at the Manor years ago – she'd love to see what's going on.'

'Steve, what I really want to know is when are *you* coming?'

'Oh, I'll come too.'

'No, no. I mean to work. Can we fix a start date?' It was Steve's turn to fuss with his dogs.

'Oh right – it's difficult this week, James.'

'What about next?'

'Should be fine – I'll give you a bell later on. All right?'

Before I had a chance to say that it was less right than anything he had said that evening he was striding off across the fields.

The next morning I suggested to the girls that we walk through the fields to look at the monks' ponds.

'Do the monks have ducks?'

'No, I don't think so. There are no ducks there now.'

'How do you know?'

'I've been finding out all about the history.'

'But they could have arrived today.' I shrugged, keen to get out.
'Daddy?'

'Yes.'

'I don't think you know much about these ponds.'

'I wouldn't say that, I've been finding out masses of stuff.' They
both looked at me.

'OK – you're right. I don't know much.'

'Can we take some crusts?'

And so we ruined a perfectly good loaf and set off across the
fields. We arrived at the ponds, hidden by undergrowth and, like so
much else here, almost invisible to the casual passer-by. These
ponds, now overlooked by a defunct railway line, had been built in
stone at a time when most of the village lived in wooden huts. Only
buildings of status used stone: churches, castles, palaces and fish
ponds . . . it did not make much sense, until I discovered that the
church decreed that on Wednesdays, Fridays and Saturdays no one
ate meat. Consequently most estates had their own fish ponds,
called stews, in which they bred carp, considered a luxury, and pike,
which was more commonplace. Tangled up somewhere in this
wilderness, so many people had lived. Were these ponds, newly
acquired by Steve, really once tended by monks?

It was about to rain, the sky and earth now joined in a solid
sheet of grey – no gaps, no answers and no ducks. Julia lobbed a
stone into the clearest patch of water, some ripples and then nothing. Once more the water was smooth and silent, except for the rain
which had started to bounce back off the surface.

I left Saltford in the powerful hands of the Bishop of Coutances.
Powerful they may have been, safe they were not. After the
Conqueror's death in 1087, Geoffrey forfeited Saltford and all his
lands after leading an unsuccessful rebellion against the new King
William II and it passed into the hands of the Duke of Gloucester.

Three years later, a boy was born whose influence on this house can still be felt today. His father was King Henry I of England. The boy's name was Robert FitzRoy, which meant 'son of a King', the name given to royal bastards, and he was to become the third owner of Saltford Manor.

Robert FitzRoy's childhood was in all probability a cold affair. William of Malmesbury, a contemporary historian, maintained of King Henry that 'his intercourse with women was undertaken not for the satisfaction of his lusts but from the desire for children. Therefore he did not condescend to intercourse unless it might produce that effect.' It did. Henry fathered more illegitimate children than any other English monarch – an estimated twenty-two. It is likely that Robert spent a great deal of time alone with his mother waiting for infrequent visits from his father who, subsequent events suggested, he adored.

Robert married Mabel, who on her father's death inherited the 'honour' of Gloucester, so called because holding a collection of lands and rights was regarded by the Normans as an 'honour'. Robert now had a title, one of the richest estates in the country which included Saltford and then, most wonderfully, a son whom he called William, in memory of his famous great-grandfather. In the years that followed they were inseparable. Robert, who never escaped the shadow of illegitimacy, lavished on William all the love that he had been denied in his boyhood and, as in many such exchanges, knew himself to be the one most blessed.

And then on 25 November 1120, everything changed. Henry's legitimate son and heir drowned at sea with the entire crew and all but one of the passengers of the *White Ship*, the fastest vessel in the royal fleet. It was the *Titanic* of its day, a celebrated ship on its maiden voyage sunk off the coast of France with the loss of nearly three hundred lives, amongst them the flower of English nobility. William of Malmesbury, not given to understatement, wrote: 'No one ship ever brought so much misery to England; none was so notorious in the history of the world.' The immediate effect on Henry was devastating. He is said to have passed out when told the news and, as every English schoolboy used to know, he never smiled again.

At that moment Robert, who as a boy had looked destined to hang around on the edge of life, became Henry's only adult son. He became Henry's constant companion and trusted counsellor, supreme in the *familiares regis*, the group of men most closely associated with the King. But behind the formality, something personal was happening. For his part Robert was perhaps able to cut through the sadness that Henry wore like a cloak, and take his father if not to a place where he could laugh, at least to a place where he could talk. The two men shared much. Henry was able to read and write – accomplishments beyond even those of the highest rank – and he had a reputation for scholarship: men called him Henry Beauclerk.

Robert also loved books. He commissioned a man called Geoffrey of Monmouth to write a remarkable book, completed in 1135, called *Historia Regum Britanniae*, the story of the kings of Britain. Its popularity was immediate and widespread and it was almost universally accepted as genuine history. There was, however, one voice of dissent. A fellow historian writing at the end of the century called Geoffrey's book *ridicula figmenta*. He had a point. For a man writing the story of England it was risky to ignore several hundred years of Anglo-Saxon occupation and make England a nation descended from classical stock. According to Geoffrey, the founder of Britain was in fact Brutus, great-grandson of Aeneas, who dropped in on his way back from the Trojan War. He also invented King Lear, borrowed to great effect by Shakespeare, and made much of King Arthur, recasting him as an emperor who 'conquered the Irish and wiped out the Scots'. Notwithstanding the romance and sheer fantasy, this book, of which fifty copies still exist today, was enormously influential. Versions of the story were translated into different languages and it is from this book that the famous Arthurian romances of Malory and Tennyson were ultimately derived. Geoffrey of Monmouth's book was a heady mix of fact and fiction, of folk tradition and fantasy, which had been thrown up in the air and cleverly placed in a contemporary setting of tournaments and love affairs; just the kind of thing that would have appealed to his patron and paymaster, a man who had spent much of his early life alone with his dreams.

Robert was a romantic but he was also a Norman, fizzing with restless energy; he would have wanted to know *everything* about his new estate. He might well have read for himself the Domesday Book. Ensconced in his father's treasury, surrounded by chests of gold and jewels, he would surely have enjoyed turning the creamy yellow parchment and reading the stylish Latin handwriting. But, for all its astonishing qualities, the facts contained in this epic survey were, by Robert's time, over thirty years old; and the man I felt I was getting to know might have wanted to see for himself the changes that had taken place on his newly acquired estate. At this time the family's main residence was Bristol. Perhaps Robert rode out with his son William to see the estate. It is perfectly possible that on one such trip, with Geoffrey of Monmouth's stories fresh in mind, they saw the ford which Arthur was said to have crossed. In any event he would have been familiar with the Manor, then, in all probability, a low wooden building.

The early years of the Conqueror's rule were characterised by almost constant rebellion and the Normans needed to secure their new kingdom. Within a generation they had built over five hundred castles, many of them hastily constructed wooden structures built on an earth mound. Windsor Castle and the Tower of London were first built in this way. But fifty years after the conquest the immediate dangers of rebellion had passed and churches began to appear everywhere. A select band of French master masons swept across the country building new churches and reconstructing Saxon ones, using the style of architecture known as Romanesque with the rounded arches favoured by the architects of the Roman Empire. Work had begun on the great cathedral buildings of Canterbury, Durham and, significantly for Saltford, Hereford. The southern transept of Hereford Cathedral had five tiers of arched windows, the most dominant of which was almost identical to the window that now graces our bedroom. It was this connection that enabled the architectural experts to date Saltford to 1148, because this was the year the windows at Hereford were completed. The same man, it was thought, had been responsible for both. But why build a window modelled on those of a great cathedral in a modest manor as unimportant as Saltford?

King Henry had died some years earlier after making it clear that he wanted his daughter Matilda, Robert's half-sister and William's aunt, to succeed him to the throne. A significant section of the barons supported another claimant called Stephen and there began one of the bloodiest periods of English history, described by a contemporary as 'the nineteen long winters when God and his angels slept'. Robert and William moved all around the country marshalling troops, at one stage capturing Stephen and taking him to Bristol. In 1139 the nearby city of Hereford, then under Stephen's control, was liberated by Robert's troops and we are told that the cathedral was used for stabling horses. Perhaps Robert and William saw the half-completed windows and returned later to see the work being finished: French masons moving across the edifice of rough timber and rope that encased the rising stonework, the afternoon sun playing across its creamy curves. Here was beauty. Sculptured stone, it must have seemed to them, shaped to perfection.

The conquest of England made the Norman elite, men like Robert and William, so rich they could build almost anything they wanted. Writing in 1142, William of Malmesbury said, 'You might see churches rise in every village, built after a style unknown before; you might behold the country flourishing with renewed rites; so that each wealthy man accounted the day lost to him which he had neglected to signalize by some munificent action.' It seemed that Robert was just such a man. The work on St Mary's church, which boasts a central Norman arch, would be his 'munificent action', fulfilling his public responsibilities; but the work on the Manor, conceived as a blunt, solid building with its feet firmly planted on the ground, would be personal. His instructions were to create something that would astonish, just as he himself had been astonished the day he had seen the work at Hereford.

And then, on 31 October 1147, less than half a year before the Saltford window was built, Robert died of a fever in Bristol. Perhaps it was William, in the winter months following his father's death, who commissioned the Saltford window as a personal memorial to his father. All we can know with certainty is that the window was crafted with breathtaking care and skill. It was the passionate work of men who wanted to light a lamp which nothing, not even their own deaths, could extinguish.

Eighteen years after the window had been completed, William was at the deathbed of his eldest son. What exactly happened in the cold halls of Cardiff Castle can, like much of this story, only ever be partially known. Perhaps the boy, hollow-eyed with fatigue, asked William to come to his bed. He must have been weak but not, apparently, too weak to ask his father to establish an abbey to pray for his soul. William, who had no time for what he had always called religious nonsense, nevertheless knelt without a moment's pause on the rush-covered floor, leant forward and kissed his son gently on the forehead. The father could not speak and the son, lapsing in and out of coma, could not hear, but both knew a promise had been made. By evening, the boy was dead.

In the days following his son's burial it would not have been surprising if William revisited Saltford to see again the window now widely regarded as fine architecture but loved by William because it reminded him, quite simply, of his own father. Perhaps you need to have looked through the window, alone at the dead of night, to see his face lit by what I imagined to be a full winter's moon, now shining, now hidden by whispers of high cloud. The furrowed fields that spread north from the house were brushed with silver glaze, the line between heaven and earth, previously so clearly defined, now strangely blurred. There was every reason to find these fields familiar, even comforting, but tonight their symmetry had been swallowed up in the cold chaos of the sky. Perhaps he understood how little he truly knew, not just about this place but about anything. He had walked across these fields many times with his father, glimpsed them briefly with his son, but now it was as if he was looking at them for the first time, staring into some future night, a never-ending blackness into which he had disappeared.

The desire to leave a signature on a patch of earth, to shape a landscape in memory of a loved one, is a common thing. Within days William had asked his cousin, now King Henry II, to establish an Augustinian monastery on a hill, visible from his window. Saltford had been owned by men whose commands were heard in the great halls and palaces of the land, but perhaps in the end the most powerful words were those whispered by a dying boy who in the last moments of his life had asked for prayer. According to its foundation charter, now in the British Museum, Keynsham Abbey was founded in 1167 because of this boy's request.

Saltford was doing what it would always do: providing a studio version of events being played out on England's main stage. The idea that God heard his special envoys, monks and clergy, more easily than ordinary mortals was central to medieval thinking. Increasing numbers of men and women were joining the newly established monastic orders, primarily Cistercian and Augustinian, which sprang up all over the country in response to what many saw as spiritual decline. But this movement took different shapes. Whilst Friar Tuck was in Sherwood Forest helping Robin Hood, the Augustinian canons at Keynsham were moving at the more mystical end of the spectrum. They belonged to an order which took vows of perpetual chastity, poverty and obedience. The day, which began at midnight, was a succession of services, manual work, chanting, reading aloud and private study, leaving little time for sleep or food. By the end of the next century it is estimated that some 20,000 people owed their livelihoods to an association with a religious house, 26 of whom were monks attached to Keynsham Abbey.

In the small unremarkable room at the top of the house, on a bed of crumbling plaster, was the fragment of a painting which had been mentioned in a newspaper cutting I had unearthed in the library. The painting was of a wheel, on one side a climbing figure and on the other the tense grip of a hand turning it. This painting, according to the art expert quoted in the newspaper article, was of a wheel of fortune, one of only five known examples of this subject. Three had been in the royal palaces of Winchester, Westminster and Clarendon, now all destroyed, the fourth can still be seen in Rochester Cathedral and the fifth was here. The Saltford fragment is the only surviving example of this subject in a domestic setting. The article suggested that the paintings, of which the wheel was only one, might prove to be the oldest domestic wall paintings in England. For me the question was not whether these paintings were *the* oldest or even *nearly* the oldest, since eight hundred years give or take the odd decade makes no difference, but rather who were the people behind these paintings?

There then emerged the next, but by no means the last, unexpected clue in the looping saga unfolding before me. No great events turned on it, no one wrote about it at the time and all that is now left are some slivers of paint on the walls of our house. Nevertheless, this wafer-thin connection took me to Winchester, a city some sixty miles south-east of Saltford.

At that time Winchester, not London, was the capital of the country. It was the place where Henry II, the Conqueror's great-grandson and William's cousin, held court. The city was important for all sorts of well-documented reasons: for example it housed the Domesday Book and it was the place where the King kept his money. But it was important to Saltford because of its paintings. Henry covered the walls of his bedchamber in his palace at Winchester with paintings. From this time on the painter followed the builder. Bare rubble or stone surfaces, like Saltford's, were considered unfinished and unworthy, but it was not always possible to have all surfaces covered in figure subjects so a great deal of ornamental painting was undertaken. The most common treatment was the masonry pattern, or painted stone joint, which explained the painted imitation wall on our top landing.

Henry's bedchamber must have been highly decorated because a monk, using an eye-witness's account, described it like this: 'It happened in a tyme at Wynchestre in this kyng Henries chambre, that was dyevrsliche i-peynted, that one place was let unpainted at the kyng's heste'. In this place Henry commissioned a mural which showed an eagle being attacked by four younger birds. Late in his reign, probably some time after 1173, he is described as staring at this painting and observing: 'Those four birds are my sons who are harrying me to death.' Throughout his reign he faced almost constant rebellion from one or more of his own family.

Winchester was also important to Keynsham Abbey because, as part of its foundation charter, the King had granted it lands just outside the north gate and land and property within the city itself. A representative from the abbey, possibly the Abbot himself, must have visited the city often to supervise the management of these important assets. Approached from the downs in the late afternoon light of a summer's day, Winchester looked majestic. The golden spire of the newly built cathedral stretched ever upwards and the massive round castle dwarfed the figures in the streets below. Rows of mud and straw huts lapped chaotically against the stone walls of the palaces and castles which had housed bishops and kings since the days of Alfred the Great. Chepe Street, Tannerestret, Scowertenestret were a constant swell of activity with butchers and bakers, tailors and drapers all proffering their wares. On street corners stall-holders sold pies, roasted finches, larks and thrushes – bought and eaten in transit. And everywhere the smell: narrow lanes littered with horse dung, butchers' offal, human excrement and daily rubbish. To a man who spent his time in cloistered silence the ebb and flow of this place might have been overwhelming or exhilarating. Perhaps it was on just such a trip that the Abbot, questioning a treasury official about land rents, first saw the Winchester paintings, or perhaps William saw them for himself. In either case the end result was the same. William of Gloucester did not just leave Saltford with a magnificent window, he left it with unique paintings.

Somehow, William commissioned an artist, possibly from a monastery, to work on the walls of Saltford. His son had died asking for prayer; perhaps he got prayer in graphic form. Certainly that is how it feels whenever I look at the Virgin and Child and the man holding what looks like an orb. As the first rays of morning sunlight appeared, the artist of these paintings looked out towards the soft red dawn that wrapped itself around Kelston Hill. The morning light made his work glow, releasing the natural mineral tones in the way that only sunlight can do. They are beautiful now; when they were freshly done they must have been sublime.

The Virgin and Child is fragmented and faded but it is just possible to make out the head and shoulders of a seated woman holding a child and to see the folds of her cloak gathered around her feet. Opposite is a clearer painting of a man's face fringed by curls. Above his head are the broken lines of what looked like a crown and in his hand is a globe, like that held by kings and queens. The medieval artist and viewer shared a visual language: hands outstretched meant the figure was asking for something; a seated figure had received a blessing; a globe and crown meant royalty. Nevertheless this painting is more than a coded sign; like the window in our bedroom it is personal. It is like a child's painting: flat, two-dimensional and utterly sincere. Who was this simple-looking man with the childlike curls, the globe and the broken crown?

His position was significant: only a saint would be worthy to face the Virgin. Saints lived in heaven, which was seen as something close to a royal court. God was the King, biddable but with a busy agenda. He intervened actively in daily life but gave priority to those who got his attention. On earth it was the professionals, the monks, who enjoyed easy access. In heaven it was the saints. Their lives had earned them a direct transfer to God's court, where, if approached correctly, they spoke on behalf of those men and women still on earth. People felt a special affinity with one particular saint because something about his or her life touched a part of their own.

In the closing decades of the twelfth century one of the most popular English saints was Edward the Confessor, the King referred to in Saltford's Domesday entry. During his reign he had built a great church, which was known as 'the west minster' to distinguish it from St Paul's, known as 'the east minster'. Edward was a tall, skinny man with white hair, reported to have had unusual skin pigmentation – suggesting he may have been an albino. This strange-looking creature with the translucent complexion who spoke Norman French and spent hours praying and reading his Bible must have seemed, to the earthy Anglo-Saxons who made up his court, something of an outsider. He was said to have had a gift of healing, touching and curing many people, especially the blind and those suffering from scrofula, a form of tuberculosis that caused swelling in the glands of the neck. The popular view of Edward, shared by William of Malmesbury, was that 'he was a man by choice devoted to God, living the life of an angel in the administration of his kingdom . . . he was so gentle he would not say a word of reproach to the meanest person'. In 1102, forty-four years after his death, the Minster monks opened his tomb and declared that his body had not decayed, a report verified by their abbot and the Bishop of Rochester. The tomb soon became the scene of many miracles and nearly a hundred years after his death, Edward became the only English King to be declared a saint by the Pope. In 1163 his body was moved by Archbishop Thomas Becket and devotion to him became so great that the dust swept from the floor of his shrine was collected and sent abroad.

Edward had lived with one foot on earth and one in heaven and his story would surely have touched William of Gloucester, just as it did many ordinary English men and women. Like them he knew pain, in his case the unspeakable anguish of a father who in 1165 had attended his son's funeral.

In one sense, this chapter of Saltford's story closes with William's own death on his birthday, 23 November 1183. But history leaks and what happens in one era affects another in ways which we never fully understand. This place is best described using the language of textures and smells; it has that indefinable 'something' which makes a house appealing. I have watched many people step across the threshold and pause, struggling to describe this quality. Ashley and Cyrille, some London friends visiting for the weekend, got closer than most.

At the bottom of the drive Ashley, seeing the house for the first time, stopped stone dead and laughed.

'Guys . . . *come on.*' He was laughing so hard he would have fallen into the trench if Cyrille had not grabbed his arm. Gasping for air, he continued, 'You're kidding me.'

By now we were all laughing. There had not been much laughter around recently and it was a relief to be with people with whom we shared some history. Someone, I think it was Anna, came back to earth first.

'What's so funny?'

'I can't believe it, you've really gone and done it. You're actually going to live *here*? Just awesome.'

'You like it?'

'I love it.'

We jumped across the trench, with them an adventure, and set off around the house. They did not seem to see all the work needing to be done and never once mentioned money despite the fact they hardly had any. Touching the wood and stroking the stone, they behaved as if they were visiting a zoo rather than a house. With them there were no hushed tweedy tones, just full-on enthusiasm.

I let them go ahead of us – enjoying seeing them discover each room for themselves. They walked into the smallest bedroom (bedroom 3), the room with the two paintings, and stood in the doorway.

'This is a nice little room.'

'Yes, but take a look at those.' I had caught up and gestured to the paintings.

'Oh my goodness – Cyrille quickly look.'

'Beautiful, really beautiful . . .' Ashley nodded, now speaking quietly. 'Just think . . .'

I told them a little of what I had found out about the paintings.

Ashley had taken up the position I loved, sitting in the well seat between the paintings. 'Don't just sleep here – do something with it.'

'Like what?'

'I dunno – just something.'

We walked into the master bedroom and stopped, our eyes drawn naturally through the stone-pink curves of the window down onto the garden below. The sun, fast falling, dropped splashes of weak winter light on the apple trees spread across the lawn. Soft blooms, glossed just for a moment. In the past, nature had often made me feel restless; here there was nowhere else to go, the circle somehow complete. It was difficult to believe that this garden had not always been this way, but William's monks had seen something very different: a busy spread of buildings which probably contained a kitchen and bakehouse, stables and farm buildings. The wood and the thatch of those buildings had long since disappeared, foundations dissolved in the earth. But now, in the stillness of a winter's afternoon, something buried had become visible, as if our presence had unlocked the afterglow of the past. And then, just as I was hoping that nothing would change and I could stay here for ever, the sun ducked down behind the trees, the light changed and the moment, always fragile, had gone.

Ashley turned, his voice just the other side of a whisper. 'Can you believe this place?'

'Only sometimes.'

'So what's the story?'

'Well . . .'

# 4

# Silence and Shadows

I N THE CLOSING YEARS of his life, William, having no male heir, gave his estate to Henry II, in return for which Henry's son, nine-year-old Prince John, soon to become King John, was to marry his daughter. And so it was that Saltford passed into the hands of a man whom school history has condemned to the 'bad' pile. In recent times there has been an attempt by some historians, eager to find a new angle, to say that he was not all bad. Isabel of Gloucester, William's daughter, would not have been persuaded. As soon as John was King he decided that he needed a wife of higher rank, the marriage was annulled and she spent fourteen years being moved from castle to castle as a state prisoner under house arrest.

Isabel was luckier than some; John was said to have hanged his next wife's admirers from her bedposts. This was not a man given to seeing the other person's point of view. During the negotiations with the barons over Magna Carta, negotiations which he came out of very badly, he returned each evening to Windsor Castle so angry that he rolled around on the floor, clawing at the air and chewing sticks, his face peppered with blue patches. He had no time for the church, always refused Communion and thought nothing of interrupting a bishop's sermon to say he wanted his breakfast, jangling the coins in his purse. And as if all this was not enough, he finished his days losing the most valuable fortune the country had ever known in the quicksands of the Wash. He had specialised in the kind of evocative disasters from which it is difficult to recover.

In writing about lives lived so long ago, I am at the very limits of what is knowable. The written clues, such as they are, are few and far between. Sir Edward Rodney, whose family were about to appear centre-stage, writing in the seventeenth century and clearly engaged in similar detective work, expressed some of the frustration I felt. 'The times are dark and cloudy, without any furniture to the argument.' The sunlit rooms left by Robert and William now seemed shadowy and bare. No clues, no Anglo-Saxon Chronicle – just the silent passage of time.

But then in 1306, when the English King, Edward I, was in Scotland fighting Robert Bruce, something happened south of the border. Saltford, always happier in the shadows, became visible again. But this time the man responsible knew nothing of palaces and kings. He was born in a tiny Somerset village into a family of tenant farmers known as 'villeins', the highest class of dependent peasantry, and was admitted to the cathedral school, where he must have impressed the authorities because they took the unusual step of granting him the freehold right to the land his family had worked for generations. Richard de Rodney, a man with a fast-track administrative career ahead of him, acquired a share in the freehold of Saltford Manor in 1306.

Richard spent his entire life in the King's service: he collected taxes, was commissioned to act as judge and to investigate the conduct of the sheriffs in Worcestershire, Herefordshire and Gloucestershire. In 1314, the year Robert Bruce trapped Edward's army in a Scottish bog beside Bannockburn and sent the English King scurrying back to England, Richard was to be found pursuing his own watery appointment as commissioner of sea walls and dykes. Bannockburn was important for Saltford. Gilbert, the seventh Earl of Gloucester, had been killed on the second day of the battle and the division of his estates, which still included a part-share of Saltford, was contested. His widow claimed to be pregnant and Hugh Despenser, married to one of the Earl's daughters, issued a writ ordering the countess be examined by discreet knights and ladies to see if her pregnancy was real. A learned committee set up to discuss this delicate matter failed to come up with an answer. It is possible that Richard might have been on that committee because the Earl's daughters appointed him as one of the trustees of their estate pending its partition.

Two years later, Richard, a man who might have expected to spend his life managing an obscure Somerset smallholding, was called to Keynsham Abbey and became a knight of the realm.

'In the name of God, St Michael and St George, I make you a knight.'

The new King, Edward II, gave Richard a blow with the flat of a sword on each of his shoulders, signifying the last insults he could receive without retaliating. Gathered around the two men were the Earl of Pembroke, who invested the sword, and the Lords Berkeley and Badlesmere, who gave the spurs. But it didn't end happily, at least not for all of them. Badlesmere was hanged as a traitor, Pembroke was 'murdered suddenly on a privy seat' and the King died in Berkeley's castle, said to have been murdered by someone with the inventive idea of shoving a red-hot meat roasting spit up his anus. In contrast Sir Richard, as he now was, moved in quieter waters. He became the King's land agent, a sort of royal estate agent cum tax collector, for the whole of England south of the River Trent and died, as far as we can tell, peacefully.

By the end of the century the poet John Gower had written:

> *The world is changed and overthrown*
> *That it is well-nigh upside down*
> *Compared with days of long ago.*

Richard had lived through a time of transition when these changes were half-complete. The old feudal system based on the exchange of land for military service had begun to give way to a system where men's ambitions were satisfied by whoever could pay for their services. Men who owned land were bound to be farmers or landlords before they were anything else and the crown needed a military force which could be paid in some fashion other than land. These changes had started to emerge within a hundred years of the Conquest but the process was accelerated during Richard's lifetime. The landowners hired soldiers to fulfill their obligations to the crown and the great houses of Warwick and York, with whom Saltford was to be associated, began to gather around them small private armies and an ever-growing household of servants and retainers. Men like Richard, effectively royal retainers, helped the crown to raise money and maintain stability during a time of political scheming and violence. As the events on England's main stage swirled around him, Richard appeared to move quietly forward, not unlike the house he was to leave to his family.

Richard's rise through the ranks of royal service took place during one of the worst famines the country had known. It began with the poor harvest of 1314, succeeded by two years of wet weather and disastrous crops. At Berwick Castle the carcasses of the dead horses were boiled by the cavalrymen, who ate all the meat and left the bones for the foot soldiers. Peasants sold small amounts of land, on average less than an acre, in order to buy food, but Richard was wealthy and, being in the pay of the crown, not reliant on the land for his income. As in any crisis there were opportunists who turned the situation to their advantage. Certainly this appeared to be the case in Saltford because in 1321, in what is the first entry in the parish register, we learn that a priest had elected himself Rector of St Mary's church. Richard, ever the lawyer, used a Norman writ called the assize of mort d'ancestor to evict the illegal tenant and installed John-de-Chewe. In the light of its spiritual heritage, it seems fitting that the last recorded act of the man whose family was to own Saltford for the next two hundred years was to replace a rogue priest with his own man. Richard died in 1322.

Saltford started its recorded life in the hands of one of the most powerful Norman families in the land, and then a little over a hundred years later, it was owned by the family of a man who had grown up in the marshes of Somerset. And yet these two men, William of Gloucester and Richard de Rodney, so different at birth, shared something in death. In 1334, some twelve years after his father's death, Richard's son Walter had his parents' bodies moved from Backwell church and reinterred in Keynsham Abbey where William of Gloucester had also chosen to be buried. One was the son of an earl, the other the son of a smallholder, but briefly, for the blinking of an eye, they had shared Saltford.

In 1331 Walter's name appeared together with that of Roger de Brikebeke, a clerk in the Bishop's household, accused by the Archbishop of Canterbury of 'doing violence' to his servants at the door of the chamber assigned to him during his visitation to Glastonbury Abbey. Difficult to imagine his father, who had worked his way so carefully up the various political ladders, getting into a fight with anyone's servants, still less those of the most powerful churchman in the land. But whatever the truth behind the brawl at Glastonbury, Walter managed to perform his local duties satisfactorily enough. Two years after moving his parents' bodies he appointed Lord William of Winchester to be Rector of Saltford.

It appears that William was one of the many absentee rectors who regarded parishes as tradable assets. This could be a lucrative business, so lucrative that by the end of the century there were brokers dealing in priests' benefices. The absentee rector took the 'tithe', a tax consisting of a tenth of all the produce from several parishes, and appointed deputies to do the real work. This seems to be what happened at Saltford, because two years after appointing Lord William, Walter appointed Thomas Sampson as his assistant. In a tiny parish this would not have been necessary unless William was absent. Thomas, so the parish records tell us, 'had the first tonsure', which meant he had just had a ring cut out of the centre of his hair to give him the appearance of a man of God. He was probably a village boy who had started, to the delight of his pious mother, as a server to the village priest, and 'the first tonsure' would have marked his intention to enter the ranks of minor clergy. Such men encouraged and consoled, they were with the villagers in the great moments of life and death, and for better or worse they were the parson – that is *the person* – of the village.

The year 1348 was a dangerous one to be a parish priest, especially one who visited the sick. In the late summer, black rats carrying a disease, known to us as the Black Death, entered the South-West of England through ports such as Weymouth and Bristol. When the rats died their hungry fleas moved on to human beings and infected their new hosts when they bit them. The bubonic plague was a warm-weather disease, most active in summer, but in the winter it developed an even more deadly pneumonic strain which could be spread directly from person to person by coughing. From the flea's point of view, the conditions could hardly have been better. Cartloads of hay and grain took the rats from their point of disembarkation to a random inland destination where they found comfortable lodgings in the straw and thatch buildings of every town and village. Within months the country was gripped by a plague of biblical proportions. 'It passed rapidly from place to place,' wrote the Registrar of the Court of Canterbury, 'swiftly killing ere mid-day many who in the morning had been well.'

One of the most terrifying things about the Black Death must have been that everyone could see it coming. 'It ravaged Somerset up to Bristol' – this sentence is one of thousands written by contemporaries, lost within the dusty leather-bound depths of the British Library. It is accurate and consistent with other evidence but does not describe what it must have been like to be living in Saltford in the autumn of 1348, hearing that a disease which wiped out whole communities apparently within hours was creeping inevitably towards you. Although movement between villages was at a minimum, they probably heard that 'the people of Gloucester denied admission to the people of Bristol, believing that the breath of those who had lived with the dying would be infectious. But in the end Gloucester, and then Oxford and then London too, and finally the whole of England were so violently attacked that scarcely a tenth of either sex survived.'

The spread of the disease through a tightly knit community like Saltford would have been further helped by neighbours entering houses to visit the sick, mourn the dead and comfort the bereaved. A Welsh poet called Euan Gethin described his symptoms:

> Woe is me of the shilling in the armpit. It is seething, terrible, wherever it may come, a head that gives pain and causes a loud cry, a burden carried under the arms, a painful angry knob, a white lump. It is of the form of an apple, like the head of an onion, a small boil that spares no one. Great is its seething, like a burning cinder, a grievous thing of an ashy colour.

The disease attacked the lymph glands in the armpits and groin, causing them to swell – hence the apples and onions – and finally to burst beneath the skin. Victims suffered high fever and unquenchable thirst, often tearing off their clothes and throwing themselves into a nearby stream or river, gulping huge quantities of water. The Shallows would have been ideal. 'The sick are served by their kinsfolk as dogs would be. Food is put near the bed for the sick to eat and drink, after which all fly.' All, that is, except the clergy, 45 per cent of whom died in the initial attack of 1348 and 1349. Impossible to know what became of Thomas, but within weeks Walter was pressing a new man to be the priest of St Mary's church.

On 10 January 1349 Thomas's boss, the Bishop of Bath and Wells, addressed the surviving clergy in his diocese, saying that because priests cannot be found 'for love or money' they should tell everyone in their parishes to make confession of their sins, according to the teaching of the apostle, to any lay person. The reference to money was not just rhetorical. Thomas had probably cost Walter £4 or £5 a year, the new man would have been offered £20. But at a time when 'Hardly anyone dared to have anything to do with the sick', it was difficult to find men at any price. 'Everyone', continues the same writer, 'fled from the things left by the dead, which had once been precious but were now poisonous to health . . . men and women carried the bodies of their own little ones to church on their shoulders and threw them into mass graves, from which arose such a stink that it was barely possible for anyone to go past a churchyard.' If this is accurate, and the numerous contemporary accounts suggest it was, then Walter and his family may well have fled. When the churchyards became inadequate, because either they were full or the smell was overpowering, fields were used for burial.

Fifty years ago, a drain was being dug in a field now belonging to a farm overlooking the Shallows and a large pit was found, thought to be the village burial site for the victims of what contemporary writers called the 'Great Mortality'. The bed of quicklime had left only a collection of teeth.

# · 5 ·

# Walter's Fireplace

I TRIED TO MAKE myself useful, doing the kinds of things that the builders thought a complete waste of time, like sweeping up. After a few weeks I abandoned the brush and decided to clean the oak mantelpiece in the drawing room, which, second only to the window in the master bedroom, was the feature I found the most beguiling. I began in the home decoration aisle at Homebase, giving the sales assistant what I thought was a compelling account of the mantelpiece's background history. He did not seem to grasp the full significance of what I was trying to do but recommended a large tin of a dangerous substance called Nitromors, huge bundles of wire wool and some industrial-strength rubber gloves. I wanted to find out from the cashier whether these products were safe but succeeded only in getting into a dispute about the validity of my saver card.

As the wipers swept the soft drizzle from my screen and I crawled along the Lower Bristol Road, I had to accept that the product-buying phase of restoration had been disappointing. Anna had made it clear that she thought the venture a complete waste of time. Surely she could see that it would be wonderful to strip back all the years of grime and see the original wood? She would tilt her head slightly to one side, and smile faintly. Nevertheless, I now had what turned out to be an appropriate set of basic equipment and was determined to begin. I was fascinated to see what this beautiful piece of English oak might have looked like in the early years of the 1400s, when it was first installed. It was covered with what must have been years, possibly even centuries, of grime and filth.

The process of applying toxic jelly and scraping it off, before starting the wretched business all over again, has nothing whatsoever to recommend it. It is dirty, potentially dangerous and mind-numbingly boring. And yet something happens in the act of cleaning – and arguably in some small way restoring – work which someone spent months of their life creating. It's as if the hours of physical touch that the work requires unlock something within the object. A central four-leafed shape was framed by a long run of what looked like wooden church windows, each of which was crowned by a tiny version of the same four-leafed shape. Above this central run of carving, the wood folded in a sequence of pleasing curves which flowed naturally into the flat surface of the mantelpiece. After a week of smearing, scraping and scouring, I discovered the small expansion gaps that must have been left to allow it to move without cracking. I marvelled at the subtle curves which mirrored exactly the curves of the stone columns on which it sat. But mostly I lost myself in the ebb and flow of the grain and colour – mellow, like liquid honey.

It was not difficult to imagine the new Walter de Rodney, Richard's great-grandson, in front of this mantelpiece. I saw him backlit by the orange glow of a crackling log fire, standing in the time-honoured position of house-owners down the ages, warming the backs of his legs. Walter's story, and that of the house itself, began to emerge in his father's will, written on 22 June 1417.

> I, John de Rodney, esquire, make my will in this manner, to wit, on Thursday the Feast of St. Mary Magdelene, A.D. 1417, and 5 Henry VI.
> I bequeath my body to be buried as God has ordained.
> Item. To Tristram Guynhere, 40s,
> Item. To William Anderum, 40s.
> To John Rooke, 100s.
> Item, I will that Agnes my wife, John Walsshe, Rector of the church of Saltforde and John Rooke, shall pay my debts out of the residue of my goods not bequeathed; and that they shall receive from Jon Seint Jon 250 marks which he owes me, and shall keep it for the child to be born to me, if God will it shall be born into the world; and if it die before it come to full (perfectam) age, then I will that Walter Rodney, my son, shall have of the said money 100li and my wife shall have 100 marks.

> Also I will that my feoffees the which beth seised of all
> my landys and rents in the schyre of Somerset do ther
> wyth as syre John, the parson of Salforde, and John
> Rooke, whom I make my executors, shalle Certifye ham in
> my be-halve, for Y haue declared my wylle and mym
> entent to ham.
>     In witness wherof I have affixed my seal.

The experts date the carving on the oak mantelpiece together with
other structural timberwork to the third or fourth decade of the
1400s. Walter, the son mentioned in this will, owned the house
from 1420 to 1466, which means that he was indisputably the man
responsible for reshaping Saltford for the second time.

His father's will was signed on Thursday, the Feast of Saint
Mary Magdalene, which in 1417 fell on 22 June. This was the
name day of the saint to whom the church next door was dedicated
and was an important day in Saltford's community calendar which
would have begun in the church. With no seats or pews, the congregation would have stood throughout, except for John de Rodney
and his family who sat in the reserved seats behind the chancel
screen. The priest would have stood in front of the altar with his
back to the congregation, chanting the Latin liturgy which no one
understood and only those at the front would have heard. In a
small village church like St Mary's, it is likely that the level of background chatter would have been high.

There were few who, if pressed, were not frightened by the
thought of what the devil and his army of freelance agents might
do to them. Most came week after week, probably not because they
loved church but rather because this was how things had always
been. At one level it might have felt comforting to step inside a
building so much more solid and secure than their own houses. In
this place God and John Walshe were in charge and everything was
as it should be. At least they hoped so.

I imagined the bread being held high. Now, perhaps for the first
time, the background noise was replaced by silence, as even the most
irreverent knew this to be the moment when in some mysterious way
Christ's body was made new. The unbelieving men propped against
the door at the back of the church touched their rabbits' feet, knelt

and crossed themselves twice – just in case. The wine was no sooner lowered than some of those closest to the back slipped away. Their duty had been done and there were more exciting things to do. For as long as anyone could remember, on this the feast day of St Mary, there had been a meal and a fair on the green outside the church. In common with many villages and towns across medieval England, the Saltford feast day started as a holy day and had become a holiday.

Visible at the bottom of the will is the shadow of what must once have been a thin cake of wax which carried the impression of John de Rodney's family signet ring. In the event he did not die until January 1420, by which time John Walshe, the rector mentioned in the will, had also died. Was it purely a coincidence that the two men died within months of each other? Or was Saltford revisited by one of the outbreaks of the plague which cursed most parts of England once every ten years until well after 1500?

Like most old documents this will appeared to be written in code. Who were Tristram Guynhere and William Anderum and what was the nature of their relationship with John de Rodney? These men have left nothing apart from their names, but in the fifteenth century names were significant and certainly provided a useful handle when trying to place their owners within some geographical context. During these years Bristol was developing trade links with Ireland and Iceland and it seemed possible, even likely, that these two men armed with their Nordic/Celtic names were commercial associates of John's, people to whom he felt indebted. And who was Jon Seint Jon who owed him 250 marks? It was a huge sum, four times what a skilled craftsman could reasonably expect to earn in a lifetime. This much was clear: Walter's father was a commercial man who dealt in large sums of money.

Richard de Rodney had lived in times when the feudal structures had begun to creak; Walter de Rodney lived when they were cracking. At the end of the thirteenth century, the increasing population pressed hard on the available land, labour was cheap and landowners found it easy to enforce the burdens of villeinage, burdens from which Richard had escaped. Now the process was reversed. The relationship between land and income was changing rapidly. The Black Death had caused the population to decline, which meant that the markets for farm produce also declined. Land which had been broken up by the plough was allowed to return to grass and it was difficult to find tenants. Now labour not land was precious. Serfdom collapsed as landowners found it impossible to enforce duties on men who could always escape elsewhere. On the whole it was the upper classes, men one layer above Walter, who were losing out; peasants could exploit their rarity value and get land on very advantageous terms. A new order was emerging, built by men who had neither the same commitments nor the same expenses as their betters – men like the De Rodneys.

At the same time there was a growing demand for English wool on the Continent and the wool merchants were making fortunes. The great advantage for families with large estates lay in the small number of workers required to look after flocks of sheep compared to the larger numbers needed to cultivate and harvest crops. For example, at the end of the century John Spenser, who began his career below the gentry, accumulated a string of lands on the Warwickshire borders formed from the grassed-over commons of deserted villages, which he turned over to pasture for sheep. Five hundred years later his country seat, the Manor of Althorp, was the childhood home of Lady Diana Spencer, future Princess of Wales. No documents exist to prove whether or not Walter embraced the wool trade but we do have his father's will from 1417 and his will made in 1467. The estate Walter inherited consisted of 4 manors and 40 acres and the one he left consisted of 14 manors and 90 acres. The figures tell their own story. It is almost certain that like all purchasers of cheap land during these years Walter was turning his over to sheep. There was a wave of enterprise and innovation sweeping through the rural economy, which many of the families newly arrived on the lower levels of landed gentry, like the Rodneys, were able to embrace. They were not saddled with 'old order' ideas; it was just over a hundred years earlier that Walter's famous ancestor had emerged from the damp obscurity of the Somerset marshes.

Henry V, crowned in a violent snowstorm in April 1413, was a soldier King. He came to the throne in a blaze of enthusiasm, encouraging the gentry to believe that they could add to their shrinking incomes by participating in the war against France, a war that the young King's great-grandfather had promised would last for a hundred years. As well as all the usual rewards of plunder and ransom there was, after Henry had taken Normandy in 1415, the new incentive of more land and new titles, bringing with them more money.

John Fastolf, who rose from modest beginnings to become a war hero, was one of many men who set off with the warrior King to seek fame and fortune. He got both but not at the same time. His daring exploits on the battlefields made it possible for him to buy Castle Combe, which brought him an annual income of £1,000 per year. The fame came much later, courtesy of Shakespeare. But stories get changed in the telling and the war hero called Fastolf became a bombastic coward named Falstaff. Perhaps it was just as well that by the time this version appeared on the stages of Elizabethan London the real man had been dead for more than a hundred years. Although luckier than most, the real John Fastolf, like John Spenser in Warwickshire, was a typical product of a time when it was possible to break through the ceilings of crumbling feudalism and arrive very quickly at a new social and economic level.

The story of Castle Combe, some ten miles from Saltford, is a good example of how this newly emerging wool industry could transform a sleepy hamlet into a thriving community. It was a story repeated, in less dramatic fashion, across many parts of the West Country. Villages like Chipping Campden and Fairford in Gloucestershire and Tiverton in Devon became booming country towns. By the end of the century Tiverton, now a small town in inland Devon, was amongst the fifty wealthiest and most populated English towns. Sheep were big business and there followed a golden period of building in the places where the wool trade brought new prosperity. Towns like Winchcombe and Cirencester in the Cotswolds and Stamford in Lincolnshire owe much of their charm to the 'wool-churches' that were built during this time. This was also the great age of timber roof construction with simple rafter roofs being replaced by decorative ribs and bosses, a form particularly popular in the West Country and known as the wagon or barrel roof. Fixed seating was becoming normal, which together with rood screens, another feature of West Country churches, meant that wood carving reached new heights, and these techniques spilt over into domestic architecture. The reason Walter's oak mantelpiece contained what looked like a long run of tiny church windows was that the man who carved it had probably spent most of his working life in churches.

The house that Walter inherited was austere and masculine. Not much had changed in two hundred years. The wooden outbuildings, which probably only consisted of stables and a kitchen, may well have grown to include a brewery, a bakery, possibly a laundry. Food was prepared in wooden buildings outside and brought up the outer staircase, which meant it was difficult to keep hot. The animals and grains were still kept on the ground floor and all other living took place in the first-floor hall just as it had done in Robert's time. The hall itself was what we would now call a multifunctional open-plan space, serving as local court, dining room and communal bedroom. After dinner the lord and his family would retire to his private room (the solar with the sun-soaked wall paintings), leaving the household and guests to clear away the trestle tables and lie down to sleep on rollaway straw mats placed around the edge of the hall. Herbs were strewn on the floor with straw to help make the air smell sweet. Lavender was particularly popular because walking on it released its scent and it had the added advantage of keeping away fleas.

Walter was familiar with the new houses being built in London, all of which had rooms dedicated to a particular function: sleeping, eating or sitting. They had fires with chimneys, often built against an end wall, to draw the smoke upwards. And, above all, they had more windows. The twin panes of William's window and the window in the solar were narrow because they could only be protected by canvas or wooden shutters. The expense of making glass had allowed only for the glazing of the upper part of windows, but now that had changed. Saltford must have seemed cold and dark at a time when the movement was towards warmth and light.

Walter's design for Saltford was bold: he was going to horizontally divide the high-roofed hall into two floors, putting in fine carved beams to support the new second floor. He planned to use some huge oak A-frames, like those being used in tithe barns, to create a loft space above the ceiling of the hall which could be used as secondary domestic space. The hall would also be split vertically. The east-facing solar, decorated with the monks' sun-soaked wall paintings, was to be the master bedchamber, and the heavy curtain which had separated it from the rest of the living space would be replaced by an oak partition of the kind being used in all the new houses. The area beneath the hall, for over two hundred years full of grain and animals, would be converted for use as a winter parlour, used by the family to take their meals in during the cold winter. For the first time the ground floor would have a domestic use and a stone spiral staircase would connect this new space with the first floor. Although England was a safer country than when Robert had owned the house, it was still dangerous and spiral staircases were fashionable because they helped occupants overwhelm unwelcome intruders. The new staircase rose in a clockwise direction, which meant that Walter, when defending the first floor, would have his right sword arm free of masonry. Robert's hall had been one massive room lit by a beautiful window, but Walter's house would have six smaller rooms and a fashionable enclosed chimney. This house would be warm and comfortable.

I wondered what thoughts might have been running through Walter's mind as he embarked upon such a huge project and I found myself identifying with this man. Like me he almost certainly decided to spend a lot of money without knowing exactly what he was going to get for it. The cost of transforming the house would have been more than a master carpenter could hope to earn in a lifetime. Even for a wealthy man like Walter this was a tidy sum. After a good day he probably reassured himself that he had made the right decision. It was prudent, surely, to spend his hard-earned money on restoring a house for his family. But as the time for the builders' arrival grew closer, this argument probably seemed less persuasive.

The Walter of my imagination was an anxious man with short fingernails, which said more about me than it did about him. As I lay awake at night worrying about interest rates and their effect on the property market, it was rather comforting to think of Walter lying awake in the same place with the same anxieties. Newspaper headlines like 'Property Prices Crash' would send me into a downward spiral. For Walter it would have been the fear, widely accepted amongst the middle classes, that the military campaigns in France would mean higher taxes. Taxes were granted by Parliament and were for the most part accepted as necessary. In time of peace taxes were fixed, being based on the valuation of land and moveable goods, and were collected by local people operating under the sheriffs (the shire reeves), who themselves were under men like Walter's upwardly mobile ancestor, Sir Richard de Rodney. But all that changed in time of war, when direct taxes were raised in addition to property and land taxes. These taxes were unpredictable and highly unpopular, especially with the men whom they were designed to hit hardest – the newly emerging class, like Walter.

From Walter's night-time perspective, the astonishing victory at Agincourt in 1415 must have seemed a personal disaster. Shakespeare was not thinking of men like Walter when he imagined Henry inspiring his troops on the eve of battle:

> *And gentlemen in England now a-bed*
> *Shall think themselves accursed they were not here*

In the sleepless nights that I imagined dogged Walter, he might have thought of himself as 'accursed', but for rather different reasons. He had no desire to charge unto the breach at Harfleur or anywhere else. Indeed, the only breach I imagined him worrying about was the one he could see opening up in his finances.

The expenses of the Agincourt campaign had not been paid off and the King owed huge sums to private individuals. In 1415 the City of London had been happy to advance £6,000 to help pay for the war but four years later the most it would lend, and grudgingly at that, was £2,000. In the last week of February 1421 Henry came to Bristol to start what was effectively a fund-raising tour of the country. The royal party must have ridden alongside the Shallows and up what is now Avon Lane because the Bristol road, then just a muddy lane, passed through Saltford.

Within ten years another army had gathered in Saltford, at whose head were a master carpenter and master mason. Masons were a cross between a site foreman and an architect and moved around the country working on special commissions. Under them would have been a large, locally recruited band of foot soldiers – brekmasons – who broke and cut stone; rughmasons – who built foundations and rubble core walls; freemasons – who worked in dressed stone; plumbers – for the construction of indoor washing facilities and a newly fashionable privy; and blacksmiths – for making various tools on site. It was probable that amongst the workforce would have been a John Mason, a John Plommer and a John Smyth. In the fifteenth century men were named, quite literally, after their occupation.

Two weeks after the campaign had started, the house was held captive by a tangle of ropes and scaffolding, almost defeated. The air would have been heavy with the smell of limestone spilling out of the quicklime kilns. Men carried leather pails to the freemasons laying segments of stone to form the new spiral staircase, spreading the hot lime on each new layer of stone, taking care not to slop it on their skin. I could hear the dry rasp of a two-handed saw cutting through a huge oak which was straddled across a pit to make the cutting angle easier. Four men were holding the saw: one pair at the bottom of the pit and one at ground level. I could see the broken, gaping holes where there had once been solid walls and master craftsmen waving their arms, shouting commands, forever showing their plans to men who listened intently and then promptly forgot everything they had heard. It is likely that one in every three men in the village would have worked on the site at some point during the work. They came not because of the flowering of English architecture but because they were given three pence at the end of every day.

Walter had an army – I had Mike, the Australians and a softly spoken carpenter called Russ. One morning, after an unusually sleepless night, I walked into the drawing room to find the four of them sitting on bags of cement lighting a fire in Walter's fireplace with bits of rotten elm floorboard. Mike, casual at the best of times, was wearing only a pair of beach shorts and Dr Martens. He looked less like a military commander than ever. As for recruiting an army of villagers, he said that no one in Saltford wanted to work, which was why he always went to the Backpackers Hostel. It might, I suppose, have been just possible to see the Australians as a new breed of international mercenaries, but only if I ignored the 'Ban the Bomb' emblems and 'Make Love Not War' stickers on their rucksacks.

Russ had just delivered what he called the kitchen carcassing. These were the individual kitchen units minus the worktop. I had spent days designing these and now after weeks of discussion they had arrived. The tower of unremarkable wooden units dumped casually one on top of another made the cheapest MFI kitchen look stunning by comparison. Even the Australians, who could usually be relied upon to say something encouraging, asked me what I was going to do with them. But I had not completely lost heart. I had planned to put what was left of the kitchen budget into a custom-built beech worktop which was scheduled to arrive the next day.

Early the next morning the lorry from London arrived but was too big to get up Saltford High Street, never mind the drive, and because I was the only person on site and looked like a builder, the driver asked me if I would help him unload the timber. Together we walked the first piece up the narrow High Street, past what had once been the village school and round the corner towards the house. My partner paused at the gates, carefully placing his end of the heavy timber on the ground, before continuing up the drive.

'They're spending some money on this place.'

'Mmm . . . Have you seen them?' I paused, fatally as it turned out.

'Developers?'

'Uhh no . . . I mean it's not like that.'

'I know . . . says he's doing it for the wife and kids.'

'I think he really is.'

'I know, they all say that, keeps the locals happy. Next up, he runs out of cash and he's down the plughole. Seen it again and again.'

'Really?'

'Yeah – last place I saw like this, delivered a worktop, six months later I was back with another. Turned out the place was infested with death-watch beetle. Every single new piece of timber was shot through with 'em and all for what? – a few creaky floorboards and wonky walls.'

'Right.'

'Hold up, mate, we need to flip it around.' We wrestled the massive piece of wood over the trench outside the front door, across the threshold and left it propped against Russ's kitchen carcasses (a word heavy with new meaning). As we were strolling back down the drive, he stopped and turned to look at the house encased in scaffolding.

'You know what I'd do with this?' He gestured to the front garden, the enchanted wilderness that had captured my heart on that memorable first day. 'Tarmac it.'

'Ah – and the house?'

'Pull it down. It's too old.'

Later that same day I returned to the house to find Mike and the Australians, together with Russ, happily huddled around a roaring fire framed by Walter's fireplace. The Australians were lost in the yellow copy of the *Daily Express* that they had found under the crumbling elm boards taken from a floor laid by Walter's carpenters. Above the newly cleaned oak lintel was the ornate plasterwork with the various initials and the date 1645; underneath a finger had written in the thick dust 'Happy Birthday Russ – 1998'. The flames danced their ancient dance, elm boards and beech offcuts now as one in the deep orange glow.

# 6

# John's Kitchen

THE TUDOR AGE began on 7 August 1483, when Henry
Tudor landed at Milford Haven at the head of an army of
2,000 soldiers, intending to make himself King of England.
By the time it had run its course, Columbus had discovered
America, Shakespeare had written *Hamlet* and Saltford Manor had
an inside kitchen.

In the late summer of 1476, some seven years before Henry
Tudor made his entrance, Saltford needed a new priest; hardly a
matter of great historical significance. The ceremony was probably
a routine affair, but the cast was stellar. The presiding bishop was
the Lord Chancellor of England, and the man presenting the new
candidate was George Plantagenet, the Duke of Clarence – one of
the key figures in the War of the Roses, the long-running series of
battles and skirmishes between the great houses of York and
Lancaster. Eighteen months later the Duke, better known for his
death than his life, was executed in the Tower of London, said by
Shakespeare to have drowned in a butt of malmsey wine.

Saltford was up to its old tricks. It had been quietly ticking over,
Rodney following Rodney, and then, with immaculate timing, just
when a new epoch was about to dawn, it provided the setting for
this enigmatic little cameo sequence. Why was the Duke of
Clarence, a man who had once fashioned himself as a potential
King, concerned with the affairs of a village populated by a few
hundred people? At one level the question is easily answered.
Saltford's owner had died in 1469, leaving nine-year-old John as his
heir. At sixteen the boy was too young to present a new priest and
so his feudal overlord, the Duke of Clarence, was required to perform the task. But this was only part of the story.

Saltford was now a part of the Warwick estate, which meant that the boy's father owed his feudal allegiance to one of the most powerful men in England, a man known as 'Warwick the Kingmaker'. The companies formed to fight in France had been bound together by service to the nobles who were paying their wages; when the wars in France were over it did not take long for the employers, men like Warwick, to use the same men in pursuit of their own ambitions. And no one was more ambitious than the tall, good-looking Duke of Clarence.

In July 1469 Clarence married Warwick's daughter and in so doing wrote himself into Saltford's story. Later that same year Thomas de Rodney died, leaving Saltford to John, his nine-year-old son. And so, some seven years after Thomas's death, we arrive back full circle with Clarence in Wells Cathedral presenting Saltford's new priest. It seems unlikely that Clarence, a man with hundreds of estates, would have got involved in one of the smallest merely to fulfill what he would have regarded as a tiresome minor duty. Perhaps behind these circumstances there was a subtext, an undisclosed story which makes sense of the visible action.

Let's suppose, just for a moment, that Clarence took the boy into his household. It was common practice for the sons of good families to spend part of their childhood within the household of a great lord. Clarence's household probably contained as many as 250 paid retainers, a community which included chaplains, soldiers, stewards, lawyers, grooms, cooks and kitchen boys. There were two sides to this new type of 'household' feudalism. A lord needed, for the preservation of his 'worship', to be seen to be served by well-born men. It was by the number of these dependants, by the cut of their cloth, by the fullness of the hospitality, that the public standing of a man was to be judged. A lord's reputation turned, to a large extent, on the size and magnificence of his retinue, all proudly sporting his badge. Clarence's was a chained bear. And for their part young men, like John, would have been engaged as squires carving their master's meat, filling his cup, even making his bed – all good training in the highly esteemed art of etiquette and hospitality.

And just as it does today, hospitality meant food.

# JOHN'S KITCHEN

*Sing a song of sixpence, a pocket full of rye,*
*Four and twenty blackbirds baked in a pie,*
*When the pie was opened, the birds began to sing,*
*Oh, wasn't that a dainty dish to set before the King?*

These words are thought to describe a banquet at which an enormous pie was presented and when it was cut, twenty-four musicians emerged to play for the guests. Big was beautiful. Contemporary books were stuffed full of dishes: 'Swanne with Galendine', a thickened spiced red wine sauce, 'Capons with whole Geese rost', and a 'Pecocke in his Hakell', which meant a peacock served in full plumage. The bird was first carefully skinned, feathers and all, and the flesh was then cooked and allowed to cool before being covered with a spare jacket-like skin and feathers kept in the kitchen especially for dressing. Presentation was everything: a minstrel fanfare alerted the guests that something was about to happen, and the bird in its best-wear 'jacket' was carried slowly up the length of the whole hall, held high on a gold platter as if sitting on its nest. Inches below the gilded comb resting on its proud head was a skewer thrust through the mouth, down the throat into the breast. The remains of each course, called 'manners', were distributed to the armies of servants, assistant cooks, scullions, spitboys, potboys and bottle washers who scuttled around behind the scenes. These 'manners' were either good or bad, according to the amount left. John de Rodney's manners would, I think, have been good.

For John, service in Clarence's household would have opened up a world of possibilities. A great household required a formal administrative structure, with a person responsible for each area of household life – marshal of the stables, marshal of the hall, master cook and so on. There were separate accounts kept for the kitchen, the cellar and the pantry. Being part of a great house gave those lucky enough to be selected the chance to train in what was effectively a career, in which they could expect to be kept as befitted their place in society, as well as be paid a decent wage. Frugality – especially frugality in the treatment of trusted servants, and the Rodneys were certainly that – was not considered a virtue. Openness of heart and a generous spirit were virtues to which the wealthy and

well-born aspired. At Christmas the lord would distribute sumptu-
ous robes, sometimes trimmed with fur, bearing his livery badge.
There were children and animals, music and jesters, and always
plenty of food: gingerbread, jellies set in coloured stripes, reddened
custards. For a boy, visiting such a household, even for a short time,
must have been fun.

But the house was more than just a home, it was also the headquarters of a sphere of influence, which was why so much of it was
designed to impress. And so, not surprisingly, there was a great deal
of building. The great families were spending huge sums of money
making the bleak halls and castles of their fathers more comfortable,
adding kitchens, winter parlours (like the one added by Walter) and
a range of bedchambers and apartments with windows and hearths
encased by chimneys. Up and down the country, knights and lesser
men were doing the same thing, and now, it seems, Saltford was
back up to speed. In the closing decade of the century John Rodney,
now a prosperous merchant in his early thirties, planned to add a
two-storey wing to the east gable end of the original Norman structure. The ground floor would contain a kitchen which now, for the
first time, would be within the body of the main house. The chimney, set against the new east gable end, would draw the smoke from
the hearth into the wide shaft which continued through the upper
room. The addition of an indoor kitchen meant that the food, hot
and freshly cooked, could now be taken the few short paces across
the hall and into the winter parlour. This room, once a shelter for
animals, was to become what we now call a dining room. From this
moment on the public room would no longer be Robert's first-floor
bedchamber but rather John's ground-floor dining room.

This wave of building could not have broken with such force and
on such a scale were it not for the appearance of a new type of
builder who, true to the spirit of the age, brought with them new
techniques and a new look. Saltford's master mason, whose skill was
now in such demand, was the only man on site wearing a gown,
open at the front with short sleeves reaching down to the elbow. The
gown, like the white collar and tie in the twentieth century, was a

badge which distinguished the man who had a sedentary occupation from the labourer who wore a shorter jerkin which did not restrict his movement. The gown survives today in the clothes of the clergy, the barrister's robes, the academic gown and in the robes worn on official occasions by the local mayor.

These new robe-clad builders were businessmen, using cranes and new materials and working to more demanding schedules. But the increased efficiency was almost certainly achieved at a price. The site masons and carpenters were still skilled craftsmen, but they could no longer exercise their personal taste and judgement in quite the same way as those employed by Walter had done. Interestingly they left nothing to compare with Walter's fireplace. The size of their operations and their reputation increased the demand for their services, and men, mindful of their 'worship', boasted that they had engaged some great name to carry out their work. But John Rodney was not the boastful type. Rather the opposite.

The new building tucked itself under the shadow of Robert's high-roofed hall, unquestionably the junior partner. On an outside corner was one huge red bricklike stone, quite different from the rest of the stones. All over England buildings were going up using bricks. The brick buildings of France had attracted the attention of knights fighting there. The English word 'brick' from the French *brique* did not enter the language until 1416. Between 1440 and 1450 two and a half million bricks had been used in the building of Eton College, but Saltford, true to form, had just one. The quoin stones, the technical term given to cornerstones, were especially visible and were therefore judged to be particularly important. The brick's position halfway up the south-east corner of the building gave it even more prominence. Why had the master mason chosen to use a stone which was at odds with the rest of the building?

As merchants of standing, the Rodneys had strong links with the merchant communities of Bristol, now one of the country's major ports. Two of the communities known to be strongly represented were from the cities of northern Germany and the wool merchants from Flanders, both places where bricks were in common use. And Tristram Guynhere and William Anderum, the two mystery men mentioned in Walter's will, have names which suggest they could well have been a part of these communities. These were good times for John since the wool trade with Flanders which had increased his wealth was booming. Possibly Saltford's 'great bryke' had been bought by John on a recent trip. Or perhaps John's mason, taken with the recent fashion of using bricks, had wanted to use one to give his building a new look. In either case the blues and greys of Saltford's stone gave way, momentarily, to a splash of colour.

The entrance to the kitchen, from inside the house, was through the Norman gable-end wall, all two metres of it. Candles of beeswax flickered in the gloom, weak and yellow. Facing the doorway was a deep wide fireplace and a rough oak mantle set back into the stone above the hearth. The ceiling was all wood. Two large oak beams were set into the new outer walls, now only a metre deep; and into these were set, at right angles, closely spaced connecting timbers. On top of this smoke-soaked frame sat more wood, the wide elm boards of the floor above. The only pieces of furniture were the heavy table used as a work surface, where pottage vegetables were cut up, and the chopping block for meat joints, five of which hung blood-red from the hooks still today bedded into the beam nearest the fire. Boiling was done in the cauldron hooked onto a metal pot-hanger which swung out over the fire. There were cleavers, knives and wooden mallets, special tongs for cutting sugar loaves, bunches of twigs for whisking and scouring, and pestles and mortars for grinding flesh together with the yolk of eggs and 'poudre forte', a mixture of hot spices. In the corner, there were some scouring sand and tubs for washing up. This was a room with no airs and graces; it had been built for cooking food and it did it well.

The family now ate across the hall in the winter parlour, shortly to be called the dining room. Clustered around the table set out in front of Walter's fireplace, they sat on benches and stools eating mortrew, a nutritious soup-stew, and salad. This is a recipe taken from John Russell's *Boke of Nurture*, compiled in 1460:

Salat: 'Take parsel, sawge, garlic, chilbollas, oynons, leek, borage, myntes, porrectas, fenel, and ton tressis, rew, rosemarye, pursalayne, lave, and waisshe hem clene. Pike hem, pluk hem small with thyn hond and myng hem wel with raw oile. Lay on vinegar and salt and serve it forth.'

In other words the vegetables were thinly sliced, the garlic was grated and the herbs shredded, moistened with walnut oil and sprinkled with salt and vinegar. The pewter bowl (a recent acquisition) contained a scattering of violet and borage flowers, yesterday it had been primroses. Next to the salad were two saucers, so called because they held the sauces made for the two meat dishes: a platter of pork meatballs, gilded with vibrant green parsley juice, and a platter of 'blanch mange', pounded chicken boiled with rice and milk of almonds and sweetened with honey. A pinch of sandalwood turned it pink.

The new dyeing techniques that had been developed in the wake of the booming wool trade had opened the door to a new range of colours. The walls of this newly fashionable eating room may well have been covered with tapestries bought on John's trips to Flanders. The ceiling, the underside of the boards of the first-floor hall (now a bedchamber), was painted and gilded. John may have been modest and his builder anonymous but the colours which ran through Saltford during this time were probably vibrant: greens, reds, vermilions, cobalt blue, indigo, and all shades of yellow. This was a new palette fit for an age when how things looked mattered as much as, perhaps more than, how things were.

And it was the look of a wood-burning stove as shown in a Sunday magazine article which did for me. A solid matt-black box set on a low plinth, brass handles and, this was its joy, clear glass doors behind which logs hissed and spat, crackled and glowed as if on some eco-friendly TV screen. Just looking at the photo made me feel that, in spite of all evidence to the contrary, all was indeed well. Perhaps it was the colour of the flames, warm like marmalade and whisky, perhaps the neatly collected kindling wood stacked under the plinth, perhaps the brass handles which glistened expensively or the comfortable old shoes curled on the flagstones. It looked so warm and oh so rustic. I nearly convinced myself that the allure of this stove had to do with it fitting perfectly into John's fireplace, designed to be the focal point in the room. It was the sort of image you might see in an English Heritage publication. But this does not get close to explaining why I went to sleep dreaming about the wretched thing. I *had* to have it, not another like it, just this one. Why was I, someone who normally finds it easy to resist adverts, now so totally defeated? As I reflected, I thought that it had something to do with my picture of what I was building this room for. Each age elects different rooms to be important and ours, at least the bit I inhabited, thinks of the kitchen as the heart of the house. Kitchens are all about nurture, nature, children's drawings on fridge doors and the smell of coffee. It's a dream, of course, but that doesn't stop it being powerful. Indeed, it makes it powerful. I know because I paid good money to the company which had taken this photograph, under which in capital letters the caption read: WE CARE ABOUT CLEAN AIR. This was not just a stove but a way of life.

Simon the Surveyor did not, however, deal in dreams and on every visit to the house he never failed to inspect the beam nearest the fireplace, the one holding John's five meat hooks. The end had rotted badly at the point at which it disappeared into the outside wall. It had been fixed at some earlier time but now even this repair was ineffective. With the serious face that he reserved for such announcements, Simon declared this to be a point of structural weakness which needed immediate attention. Clearly this was of the utmost importance. The solution was to get a metal socket fitted around the beam and bolt the socket to the wall. This was skilled and sensitive work and could only be carried out by a team of experienced structural engineers. The reports commissioned by the previous owner following the water damage, done by the restoration consultants fresh from Windsor Castle, said exactly the same thing. The firm Simon had in mind, with whom he had dealt for years, were coming on Saturday.

When I arrived, Brian the Decorator was washing his brushes, just about to leave.

'Hi James – how are the visions?'

Anna had told him I had a 'vision' for the children's room, the space above the kitchen. Brian had been decorating for thirty years but this, he said, in a moment that preyed on my mind, was the most ambitious thing he had ever worked on. Not that the colour scheme was ambitious: white, followed by white, topped off with a bit more white.

'So, how did it go?' I pointed to the new socket welded neatly round the end of the beam.

Brian chuckled. 'We've had some fun here.'

'Great – work should be fun.'

'No, I mean you nearly lost the place this morning.'

'Sorry?'

'Fire – the young lad who came to do that,' Brian pointed to the beam, 'hadn't got a clue. He fitted the socket, still hot, straight onto the wood. A couple of hours later Dave [the plumber] spotted smoke coming out of the girls' room. We rushed upstairs, saw the beam smoking and doused it with several buckets of water.' Brian was shaking his head gently from side to side as if enjoying a private joke. 'Seems to have done the trick but . . . close.'

'Right.' He went on to tell me how old timbers can often smoulder for days before really catching light. At least I think that is what he said, difficult to be sure because my heart was making too much noise.

'Just think . . . all the wood you've got here, the whole place could have gone.'

I walked back across the fields towards the cottage, turning every few moments to check the roofline for smoke. I determined there was only one sensible course of action. I dialled 999.

'Fire, police, or ambulance?'

'Fire – well, I hope not but I want to be sure.'

'Sorry caller: fire, police or ambulance?'

'Fire.'

'Where?'

'Saltford Manor, Saltford.'

'Postal code?'

'BS31 3EL . . . How long?'

'Ten minutes.'

I ran back, scrambled through St Mary's churchyard, no comforting peal of bells just the sing-song screech of a siren, and arrived at the gates to be met by four firemen sweeping up the drive. Together we charged in the direction of the front door and one of them pulled out his axe, preparing, I assumed, for a forced entry.

'No, really . . . I've got a key, please . . .' Taking the stairs two at a time, we were in the girls' bedroom (bedroom 2) inspecting the beam from above. At the end of an impressively thorough inspection they pronounced that there was no danger. Wonderfully they did not seem to mind at all that I had wasted their time. They wanted to have a look around so, by way of a thank you, I gave them a quick tour. It was in the kitchen, just before they left, that one of them pointed to the sharp hooks on the beam that had just been pronounced safe.

'What were they for?'

'Hanging meat.'

'Like lads who fix hot sockets onto old beams?'

Writing some six hundred years earlier, Chaucer had described one of the characters in his *Canterbury Tales* as 'a householder and that a great was he'. Chaucer went on to give his readers an insight into the man's domestic life.

> *A better envyned man was no-wher noon.*
> *With-out bake mete was never his hous,*
> *Of fish and flesh, and that so plenteous,*
> *It snewed in his hous of mete and drynke,*

Here perhaps was a model of what had happened at Saltford down the ages. At the dawning of the Tudor Age there were 500 men like John, knights who owned land. These men wanted to make their houses more comfortable, not primarily because they had pretensions to ape the great men of their time, although that clearly played a part, but because they, like Chaucer's character and, indeed, like me, wanted their houses to be places where it 'snewed' meat and drink. In short we wanted Saltford to be our home.

# 7

# Such a Candle

'TO THE KINGE our soveraigne lorde and to the lordes of his moost honourable and discrete counsel.' So began a letter from John Rodney's tenants. It was 1516. The King was Henry VIII and the 'discrete counsel' to which the tenants were appealing was the court of Star Chamber, presided over by the mighty Cardinal Wolsey, the effective ruler of England for the next fifteen years.

The letter continued: 'Pleas it your highness to understand of the wrongis oppressions and extortions doon by Sir John Rodney.' These tenants alleged that Sir John forced them to do his ploughing, and carry the wood, timber and stone he required for his building operations, not only without payment but without an allowance of food and drink, threatening to 'hang bete and mayhem them'. His red deer lay daily and nightly on their corn, and for fear of their lives they dared not drive them away. They were even forbidden to keep dogs to protect their crops. Sir John commanded his tenants to 'clog their doggis for the destroying of his dere'. A crude command and one they clearly ignored because he states that 'at certain times when their doggis troubled his dere . . . sume of his servauntis hath by chance of some stroke killed some of their doggis'.

Forced labour, flattened corn, dead dogs, the defence case was not looking good. The allegations were serious, signed as they were by thirty-three men, and so were the potential punishments. Although the Star Chamber did not use torture it could and did impose unusual punishments not available to the ordinary courts: it could fine very heavily, imprison, whip or mutilate (the loss of one or both ears was common) or put the offender in the stocks where he would be pelted with stones, offal and rotten food. And then on

3 April, inevitably given the circumstances, there was a fight, but not just any old fight. According to Sir John, one hundred and fifty 'riotouse and evil disposed persones' gathered with bats and other weapons and began to destroy some of his fences. Sir John arrived with two servants, outnumbered fifty to one; tempers flared and a scuffle broke out. This was an angry crowd because we are told that one of them had a hay fork and was, according to Sir John, 'entending to have slayne him'. The man stopped only because someone restrained him, saying, 'Let us not slee him for he is our maister.'

The timing of this letter was spot on. Only the year before, in 1515, Wolsey had begun to enforce the anti-enclosure legislation which had, until this time, proved ineffective. This was the real beginning of the move to enclose common land, a movement which was to cause such misery and starvation in the years ahead. But the men writing this letter were not thinking of such matters, they were angry and they knew exactly what they were doing. Sir John might have been their master but he wasn't Wolsey's.

The Cardinal could be seen on his way to the Star Chamber accompanied by swarms of liveried servants crying out 'Make way for my Lord's Grace!' Slowly, and with all the dignity he could muster, a well-fed man encased in scarlet silk appeared – riding on a mule. Some dared to press closer and as they did so he held a sponge soaked in vinegar and encased in orange peel just a little closer to his nose. Born the son of a butcher, he had become a man of taste. He slept softly on a bed with eight mattresses each stuffed with thirteen pounds of the finest wool. His palace at Hampton Court astonished the Venetian ambassador, who must surely have taken some impressing, with its scale – it had 280 bedrooms – and with its opulence. The ambassador estimated the value of all the gold and silver plate in the house to be 300,000 gold ducats, £75 million today. In 1516 Thomas Wolsey was at the height of his powers, combining the roles of Cardinal, Archbishop and Chancellor.

And it was to the Chancellor that John's unhappy tenants appealed. The Court of Star Chamber was theoretically supposed to be held before the King; an empty seat was reserved for his use. It was presided over by Chancellor Wolsey, who used it to humble men like Saltford's current owner who thought themselves to be above the law. Wolsey would teach them, as he put it, 'the law of Star Chamber'; which is what he almost certainly did to John Rodney. No record exists of the judgment passed but it is likely, on the evidence of similar cases, that John received a hefty fine. Sir John Rodney, who I had imagined as vulnerable aged ten, had become a bully aged fifty-five.

Behind this story was another, buried, like Saltford itself, beneath centuries of dates and dust. Why did these men feel so badly treated that they appealed to one of the highest courts in the land? There must have been more to it than flattened corn and dead dogs.

The wool trade was booming and profits were so great that men like John were turning arable land into pasture for sheep. The process had begun way back in Walter's time but now it accelerated. It appears that the common fields on John's estates used since 'tyme out of mynde' were 'nowe of late enclosed'. In common with many, John was enclosing vast swathes of land, hence the fences the crowd had been pulling down. John defended his right to erect fences on the grounds that as lord of the manor he was entitled to 'emprowe himself in his own ground'. And then as if all this was not enough and 'contrarie to all lawes and good conscience', he pulled down the houses of Mawde Jenyn and Jane Broke, two widows now left without homes. What became of these two women we cannot know. Perhaps they were left to roam the countryside grubbing for food in the woods, eventually joining the tide of homeless beggars that were sweeping into London during this time.

> *Hark hark the dogges do bark*
> *The beggars are coming to Town!*

And they came in their droves. Sir Thomas More, then Wolsey's assistant, saw 'so many poore folke at Westmynster at the dolys . . . that my self . . . haue ben fayn to ryde another waye'. More wanted to ride off in the opposite direction but took pity, got off his horse and spoke to one of them. He went on to praise the Westminster monks for providing 'dolys' or dole – a small portion of food or money given to a poor person. The numbers descending on London became so oppressive that a proclamation was issued against the armies of homeless who haunted 'the Bancke [of the Thames] and such like naughtie places', saying that they should be whipped, or burned, or imprisoned on a diet of bread and water.

The sixteenth century was no time to be homeless, which was why, of course, Sir John's tenants felt the injustices of their situation so strongly. The other possible, and more likely, fate for the two widows was that they were offered shelter, perhaps by the parson whose name appeared first at the end of the letter. Sobering and rather sad to recall that almost exactly two hundred years earlier, Richard, John's famous forefather, had emerged from a house in the shadow of Wells Cathedral which was, in all probability, not dissimilar to those his bullying offspring had recently destroyed.

One of the best-selling books of the time was a practical handbook for farmers called *The Book of Husbandry*. The author wrote for men, like Sir John, who took a keen interest in the practical affairs of farming. Addressing the farmer's wife, he says that she should 'first in the morning when thou art waked and proposed to rise, take up thy hand and bless thee and make a sign of the holy cross. In nomine patris et filii et spiritus sancti Amen.' Alongside this, the kind of thing now available to us only in exclusively devotional literature, he offered practical guidance on animal welfare. For example, if a ewe did not like one of her lambs, and was striking it with a paw, he advised tying the ewe to the side of a pen and placing a dog near the lamb in a position in which she could see it. This would awaken the ewe's motherly instincts and all would be well. It is doubtful whether such a book would ever get published today, being difficult to categorise and therefore, so the marketeers say, difficult to sell. But this one sold very well – it was first published in 1523 and nine more editions were printed over the next forty-five years. This mix of spiritual and practical, odd to us, appears to have been perfectly natural to the people of this time.

And it was the practical that the author addressed when he suggested that farmers enclose their lands and concentrate on sheep rearing: 'Shepe in mine opinion is the most profytablest cattell any man can have.' Sheep certainly were profitable, for those who could acquire land, but for those who could not, like the men who wrote this letter, they spelt ruin. They understood all too well that sheep farming meant shortage of corn, shortage of food, hunger and misery. But the man to whom they were appealing, Cardinal Wolsey, Archbishop of York, Abbot of St Albans and Bishop of Bath and Wells, cared little for anyone, far less the hungry or miserable. He had great plans and set about attacking the Church, which he thought morally corrupt, with the same reforming zeal that he had used to attack the nobility. As a prince of the Church, with a foot in both camps, he was able to do what no layman could do and transfer matters which would normally have got stuck in the Church courts directly across to the Star Chamber. Confident that all things were now possible he promised the King that he would release him from the grip of Rome and create a new Church – literally a Church of, and for, England.

And it was to this end that his agents set off to investigate some of the smaller monasteries, reported unfavourably, and dissolved them – a sort of prelude for the wholesale destruction which was shortly to take place. In July or August of 1526, his agents visited Keynsham Abbey, now the freehold owner of Saltford Manor, and found the buildings filthy and decayed, a pack of hounds wandering at will through the church and cloister, insufficient service books and a group of illiterate young canons. But perhaps the most telling indicator of the abbey's condition was this – of the fourteen canons interviewed, eight stated all was well.

Keynsham Abbey, once one of the wealthiest monasteries in Europe, had begun its inglorious slide downhill, a slide which came to its inevitable conclusion when the Abbot, on behalf of the ten monks left, signed the Deed of Surrender on 23 January 1539. In the days that followed, the church was desecrated, the lead was ripped off the abbey's roof, the seven bells were smashed and sold and the stone used to build a mansion. The furniture, windows frames, shutters and doors were sold by public auction. Within weeks the body of the church, once filled with the sound of chanting, was filled with birdsong. Keynsham Abbey, founded by William of Gloucester in memory of his beloved son, had ceased to exist and with it a part of Saltford had gone.

The house had lost its twin, the abbey, and now stood alone. In spiritual terms 1539 should have been a watershed for the house, but, as ever, nothing was quite as it seemed. Throughout the country, monks, many of whom must have profoundly disagreed with what was happening, were turned out and had to look for new vocations. For the most part they kept their thoughts to themselves, preferring an altar to silence, the parish to prison. The parish register tells the story:

> 1539  Parker Thomas
> October 25th AD in the Rectory at Saltford
> 1554  Deprivation of Thomas Parker alias Allen alias Carter.
> The deprived rector was a monk.

Saltford's rector had been a monk. In fact Thomas had been a canon at Keynsham Abbey at the time of surrender and had changed his habit, which meant that he gave up his vows to become an ordinary parish priest. He knew Saltford, may well have stayed in the house himself, and was in all probability a popular choice amongst the village. None of his sermons survive but it is reasonable to assume that he spoke in line with the current orthodoxy – namely the new flavour of English Protestantism endorsed by Henry VIII – because he married and remained as Rector of Saltford for fifteen years.

And then in 1554, one year after the Catholic Mary came to the throne, Thomas was replaced. The timing, surely, was significant. Perhaps he had changed colours from Rome to England too convincingly for the new regime. 1554 was the year when this conflict – between the Catholicism of Rome and the Protestantism of England – was being fought out in Oxford, some forty miles from Saltford, in a formal set-piece trial that was designed to discredit the entire reform movement from the 1520s onwards. The trial featured the Protestant bishops Latimer and Ridley, who refused to recant their faith. The final outcome was never in doubt.

On 16 October 1555, one year after Thomas had been removed from Saltford, Latimer and Ridley were led out from their cell. The crowd had been building up overnight and there were now upwards of two thousand people in Broad Street straining to catch their first

**Above** *The house as it was on 17 October 1997, the day we became the proud owners.*

**Below** *The 1683 hearth tax receipt until recently lost to the world but now, courtesy of June, revealed in all its glory.*

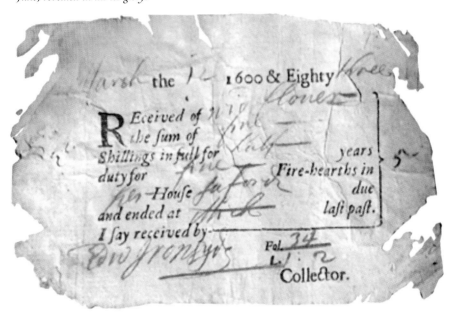

**Above** *Mike prepares to lay the new wide-gauge water pipe.*

**Below** *Ironart had done their worst – the gates are humbled, no gold letters and no lamps.*

**Above** *The upper floor of the girls' room (bedroom 2) stripped of water tanks.*

**Left** *Inside the front door, the day Anna came with curtain fabric.*

**Below** *The reception room, character but not much ceiling.*

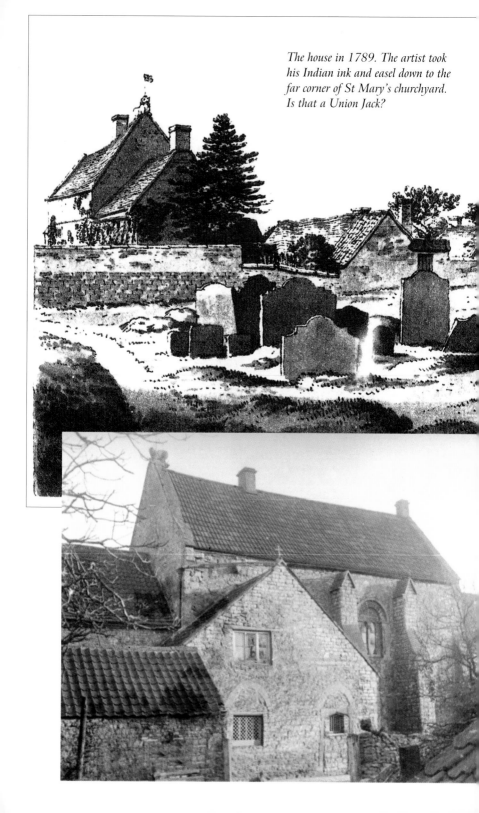

*The house in 1789. The artist took his Indian ink and easel down to the far corner of St Mary's churchyard. Is that a Union Jack?*

**Opposite**
*The back of the house, 1890. The extension with the cross on its roof, thought to have started life as an Elizabethan chapel, collapsed in the 1940s.*

**Above** *Queens School, Saltford, the class of 1902.*

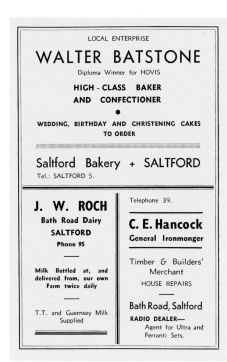

**Above** *The Scouts' booklet, 1939. No-nonsense adverts featuring local tradesmen, including J.W. Roch, whose father had lived in the Manor, and the more upmarket 'Maison Yvette'.*

**Below** *Country Life magazine, 1958. 'The Manorial Ensemble of Church and House.'*

# SALTFORD

Mid-way between the Cities of Bath and Bristol.

Particulars of an Important Freehold Property
known as

# SALTFORD MANOR FARM

comprising

The Interesting and Reputed

## 16th CENTURY MANOR HOUSE

(at present in disrepair).

Valuable Enclosures of

# BUILDING and ACCOMMODATION PASTURE LANDS

### WITH EXCELLENT SET OF FARM BUILDINGS

in all extending to about

## 20 ACRES

the whole of which, with the exception of a portion of the Farm Buildings, will be offered with

### VACANT POSSESSION ON COMPLETION.

**Above** *Estate agents' details, 1946. Noel Flowers sells a 16th Century Manor House – what happened to the previous 500 years? The next line suggests that all was not well with the house – nothing new there.*

**Right** *The Norman window dating from 1148.*

**Main picture** *The house as it is today, some ten years after we first saw it.*

glimpse of the two men. Ridley appeared first, fully robed as a bishop, with the seventy-year-old Latimer following feebly behind. They made their way forward, stopped and undressed. Ridley gave his bishop's robes and some nutmegs to those who stood close by and Latimer slipped out of his 'poor Bristol style frock all worn'. An eyewitness noted that 'though in his clothes he appeared a withered crooked old man, he now stood bolt upright . . . as comely a person to them that were there present, as one should lightly see'. As they were being secured with a chain to different sides of the same stake, Ridley's brother tied a bag of gunpowder to each of their necks. And then, as a burning torch was laid at the feet of Ridley, Latimer said, 'Be of good comfort, Master Ridley, and play the man; we shall this day light such a candle, by God's Grace in England, as I trust shall never be put out.' The following is taken from a contemporary account.

> And so the fire being kindled, when Ridley saw the fire
> flaming up towards him, he cried with a loud voice, 'Lord
> into Thy hands I commend my spirit: Lord receive my spirit!'
> and repeated the latter part often. Latimer, crying as
> vehemently on the other side of the stake, 'Father of heaven,
> receive my soul!' received the flame as if embracing it. After
> he had stroked his face with his hands, and as it were bathed
> them a little in the fire, he soon died, with very little pain.

Latimer had slipped away but it was not so with his friend Nicholas Ridley. The wood surrounding him had been piled too high and he screamed for his friends to pull off some of the wood. Misunderstanding him, his brother-in-law added more sticks to the fire. The flames 'burned clean all his nether parts, before it once touched the upper; and that made him often desire them to let the fire come unto him'. He screamed, 'I cannot burn!' And then, 'after his legs were consumed he showed that side towards us clean, shirt and all untouched with the flame'. Thomas Cranmer, a fellow reformer, with whom the two men had shared a cell, was forced to watch in anticipation of his own burning only five months away. Finally, one of those closest to him reduced the firewood and the flames licked around his face, igniting the gunpowder. The huge crowd stood as one, the crackle of firewood lost in the sound of weeping.

The despair stretched to the West Country; these were difficult days in Saltford. Latimer had chosen to wear a 'Bristol' coat to his death; he had spoken in Bristol many times and was the most out-spoken advocate of the new Protestant faith. He had many supporters and it is perfectly possible that Thomas Parker was one of them, in the light of the fact that he was removed in 1554. Thomas may well have been amongst the 800 clergy who left England in the next eighteen months, fleeing in fear of their lives and heading for cities in Germany and Switzerland, both places where the new writings of Martin Luther had taken hold.

In matters of faith ordinary people, who at the best of times were confused about what they really believed, now had the added burden of being unclear about what was acceptable. Belief, it was said, revolved with the wind. What was right during Henry's reign was wrong during Mary's. Two hundred and eighty Protestant heretics were burned in the course of three and a half years. Little wonder that a parish in Gloucestershire turned their vicar over to the authorities – just in case. And then, with the succession of the Protestant Elizabeth in 1558, the tide changed yet again. *The Book of Husbandry*, the best-selling guide for farmers, reflected what was happening. The wording of the prayers suggested for the early-rising farmer and his wife remained unchanged in the reprint of 1560 but changed in 1562. Now, instead of the wife being urged to make the sign of the cross and her husband to say a Paternoster, an Ave and a Creed, they were told 'to give thanks to God for thy night's rest and say the Lord's Prayer and other good prayers if thou canst'; and this Protestant version was reprinted in the editions of 1568 and 1598.

Spiritual movements are, by definition, difficult to see. Nevertheless, this one found physical expression, as it had done once before during William's time, but this time Saltford gained a chapel. This was the Elizabethan chapel which had collapsed some years ago, the memory of which had caused Bob the Planner such pain on our first memorable visit to the house. At the time I thought his reaction over-intense, even comic, but now it seemed exactly right. How could a building like this, which must have seen so much, be allowed to fall down? In the only photograph I had seen it was crowned with a cross, standing at right angles to John's newly constructed wing, like a holy but distant cousin. That this building existed at all implied that the owners were out of tune with the offerings available in St Mary's, less than thirty paces away, and had therefore built their own chapel. The facts were, for once, delightfully simple: the owners must have been Catholics.

A new brand of Church, known to us today as Anglicanism, had arrived and in so doing forced Catholicism underground. In 1586 the senior Jesuit priest in England was hiding in a mansion two miles from Marlow with the only two other Jesuits in the country, discussing 'our future methods of work and the prospects that lay before us'. The prospects can only have been gloomy. Of the three hundred priests who had returned during the first years of Elizabeth's reign, thirty-three had been hanged, fifty-eight had been in put in prison of whom eight had died. Priests had been landing on our shores for twelve years. Prior to this meeting in the mansion just outside Marlow – effectively a council of war organising a resistance campaign – this senior Jesuit had been making contact with Catholics who were willing to take the risk of sheltering a priest. Most of the places he visited were near London but in the summer of 1585 he is known to have been in Somerset and one of the houses on his list might well have been Saltford. In any event he gave the other two men 'the names of Catholic houses where they might go and make their residence, and arranged for reliable guides to take them there'.

Intrigues, spies, and then, some thirty years into Elizabeth's reign, an immense fleet of ships carrying tens of thousands of soldiers, the Spanish Armada, appeared off the south coast, sent from Spain with the Pope's blessing to overthrow the heretical Queen of England. But the lumbering Spanish galleons were no match for the smaller British ships and were scattered by storms in the North Sea around the coasts of Scotland and Ireland. The troops had been turned back but the defeat of the Armada did nothing to stem what many saw as a far greater threat, the Jesuits flooding into the country.

> It is known . . . that they do come into the same realm by secret creeks, and landing places, disguised both in names and persons; some in apparel as soldiers, mariners, or merchants, pretending that they have heretofore been taken prisoners, and put into galleys, and delivered. Some come in as gentlemen, with contrary names, in comely apparel, as though they had been travelling into foreign countries for knowledge . . . and many as gallants; yea in all colours, and with feathers and such like . . . far off to be thought or suspected to be friars, priests, Jesuits, or popish scholars.

Although mass in private houses was illegal, it continued, of course, to take place. But for those households without a resident priest (in other words most of the smaller houses owned by the gentry), it was a hole-in-the-corner affair. The priest came perhaps under cover of darkness, stayed for a few days and then moved on to his next appointment. Regional networks of houses joined together to form what was essentially an underground organisation and it seems that for this brief period at least, Saltford may well have been part of such a network. Setting aside the photograph of the building in the garden and the possibility that it was a chapel, there was the discovery of a huge hidden cupboard – a hole in the corner – next to Walter's fireplace. The wooden façade, split into bookcase and cupboard, was hung on a hinged frame, making it possible to open what was effectively the door to a tiny room – a 'lost' space between Robert's original outer wall and the alcove created by Walter's fireplace. Apart from hiding priests, which it almost certainly did, this space was used to hide the illegal props of the mass: candles, altar stones, sacred vessels and vestments.

Not a candle or sacred vessel in sight as we – that is Brian and Joyce, Anna and I and about six others – followed Chris the Curate meekly up the stairs of the village hall to the upper room. We had all volunteered to watch something Chris called an Alpha video – an introduction to a course which offered, it was being suggested, a chance for folk to explore the meaning of life. Chris turned off the lights and in a modern-day enactment of Moses on the shore of the Red Sea, waved the remote control airily in the direction of the TV. The waters parted to reveal the presenter, a tall slim man with twinkling eyes and a polo shirt, who quoted an article from *Private Eye* magazine, the headline of which was 'God to leave Church of England'. The article, clearly something of a scoop, went on:

> Following the example set by former leading Anglicans God has indicated that he too is to leave the Church of England. Friends of God believe the issue of women priests to be behind the Almighty's sudden decision to convert to Rome. According to sources close to God he has been unhappy for some time with the direction the Anglican Church has been taking and has now finally had enough. A Church of England spokesman said, 'Losing God is a bit of a blow, but it's just something we're going to have to live with.'

Later that evening, in the car park at the bottom of the drive, Chris asked me whether he could have the next Alpha course 'up at the Manor'.

'OK – if you think it would work.'

'Absolutely. We might even get one or two people coming just curious to see the house.'

'I hadn't thought of that but you may be right. Is that OK?'

'Sure. It'd be perfect. Your lounge would be great for the DVD.'

'You reckon? . . . I just don't see how the builders will be finished.'

'No pressure, let's just see how it goes . . . see what Anna thinks.'

The next day I asked Steve to run a digital aerial into the massive cupboard next to Walter's fireplace, ideal for a wide-screen TV because of its depth. This space, once hiding priests in fear of their lives, was now being prepared to show a talk called 'Christianity: Boring, Irrelevant and Untrue?'

# 8

# The Book of Books

I N THE LOWER south window of the nave of St Mary's church, locked away in a glass case, sits one of the earliest editions of the King James Bible. It is now more or less invisible to the people of Saltford, being shrouded in black leather to protect it from the harmful effects of the morning sunlight. But it was not always so. The book was published in 1613 and copies of it were sent out to every church in the land at the express order of King James.

The first page reads: 'The Holy Bible Conteyning the Old Testament and New, Newly Translated out of the Originall tongues: and the former Translations diligently compared and reuised by his Maiesties Speciall Commandment. Appointed to be read in Churches.' The last phrase was significant: the fifty black-robed scholars charged with this great work sat in libraries for nearly ten years poring over all 'the former Translations' because they believed that the Bible should be heard by everyone.

This translation appeared 'by his Maiesties Speciall Commandment', at a moment of optimism. Elizabeth had died in 1603 leaving unfinished business: the divide was as great as ever between the Catholics, who wanted England to return to the Roman fold, and the radical Protestants, known as Puritans, who felt that the Reformation was incomplete. King James's arrival on the throne heralded what the translators hoped would be a new beginning, a new inclusiveness flooded with light that would eclipse the shadows of priest holes and the smoke of the heretic fires. The type size of the dedication, larger than the words of the Bible text itself, hints at what is to come:

TO THE MOST
HIGH AND MIGHTIE
Prince, Iames by the grace of God
King of Great Britaine, France and Ireland
Defender of the Faith, &c.

The men engaged in this massive project saw themselves as the sub-jects of a man they called 'that sanctified Person who, under God, is the immediate author of their true happiness'. This sounded wonderful but was, of course, hopelessly unrealistic. For all the flowery language, and no one did flowery language better than the Jacobeans, the divisions between Catholic and Protestant were as great as ever and no amount of scholarly sentiment could paper over the cracks. Nevertheless the new King and God appeared nearly indistinguishable. The majesty of God can be seen, so the writer suggests, in the majesty of King James, who would steer England safely through the twin dangers of 'Popish persons at home and abroad' whose desire was to keep people 'in ignorance and darknesse' and the red-hot Puritans described as 'self-conceited brethren, who runne their own ways'. Here, right at the end of this overblown introduction, was the heart of the matter. England stood divided and Saltford, very sensibly in the circumstances, had a foot in both camps. The Rodneys, with their chapel and priest hole, were 'Popish persons at home' and the Flowers, the family about to take up residence, were 'self-conceited brethren, who runne their own ways'. But in 1604, the year when the translation was com-missioned, it was the 'Popish persons' who were centre stage.

In the small hours of the morning of 5 November 1605, a figure in a cloak and dark hat was discovered scrambling about in the cellar under the House of Lords. He gave his name as John Johnson, servant to Thomas Percy. Parliament met briefly that afternoon and the entry in the journal for the day, crammed into the margin, was as follows:

This last Night the Upper House of Parliament was searched
. . . and one Johnson, servant to Thomas Percy was there
apprehended; who had placed 36 barrels of Gunpowder in
the Vault under the House with a Purpose to blow the King,
and the whole company, when they should there assemble.

Johnson was interviewed by the King, who asked him how he could 'conspire so hideous a treason' against the royal children and so many innocent people. He simply said, with the cold logic of the fanatic, that a dangerous disease required a desperate remedy.

After the man had been transferred from the King's chamber to the Tower, the King wrote a letter which said that if he would not confess 'the gentler tortures are to be used upon him and et sic gradus ad ima tenditur', which translated means 'and so by degrees proceeding to the worst'. The King had slipped into Latin, as if the use of learned language distanced him, and perhaps even the reader, from the reality of what was about to happen. Over the next three days John Johnson became Guido Fawkes and the identity of his fellow conspirators was revealed. His signatures at the bottom of his 'confessions', declining in strength and clarity as the interrogation progressed, bear witness to what must have happened. The last one contains only his first name, a shaky scrawl, trailing child-like dabs of ink where his surname should have been.

There was something about the plot, emerging as it did from a hidden subterranean world, which threatened to overthrow the ordered world of decent Englishmen as represented by the Houses of Parliament. The shadow of the Armada, twenty thousand Catholic soldiers aboard 130 Catholic galleons, stretched over the political landscape. And now, the Protestants claimed this same enemy, dressed up in English clothing, had been caught attempting to strike at the nation's foundations.

In the hysterical atmosphere that swept through the corridors of Jacobean power in the wake of 5/11, all Catholics were potential security threats. And no one was more threatening than the Superior of the Jesuit Order in England, a saintly middle-aged man with a sweet singing voice and spectacles: Father Henry Garnet. He had known of the plotters' intentions through the confessional, and had tried, unsuccessfully as it transpired, to dissuade them from their course of action. As ever the cry for blood drowned out all other voices – the fact that most English Catholics managed to exist peaceably as law-abiding citizens counted for nothing. Catholics, so the conversations went, had excommunicated Queen Elizabeth and were in satanic communion with the Antichrist now to be found, by anyone foolish enough to go there, in Rome.

And so this softly spoken, prematurely greying man was dragged before the King and interviewed on the niceties of truth and confession. Garnet admitted he had indeed known about the plot. He was tried and found guilty of treason.

Nowhere was the cocktail of politics, religion and blood, so characteristic of these times, more evident than on the scaffold of Father Garnet. No coincidence that amongst those waiting to greet him on the scaffold, hoping for repentance and even the conversion of this famously evil man, were two of the men responsible for translating the Bible today resting in St Mary's church. Garnet knelt and prayed at the foot of the ladder he would shortly climb and then helped the hangman take off his clothes down to his undershirt, which reached almost to his feet. Mindful of this moment, he had spent some of his last hours sewing the sides together in case 'the wind might blow it up'. On the ladder he paused, making the sign of the cross, asking that all good Catholics present should pray for him. A man in the stands, hopeful that he might see a last-minute conversion to Protestantism, called out, 'Mr Garnet, it is expected you should recant.' Garnet replied, 'God forbid, I never had any such meaning, but ever meant to die a true and perfect Catholic.' Quick as a flash, one of the translators, seeing what he must have known was his last chance, said, perhaps with a half-smile, 'But Mr Garnet, we are all Catholics.'

There is, in this brief exchange, something so alien to us that it is nearly impossible to understand. Even now, with the axe and butcher's knives as witnesses, these men were warming up for yet another discussion about God. But Father Garnet was having none of it and making the sign of the cross he expressed, yet again, his horror at what the plotters had done and asked that Catholics accept their place in the kingdom and be quiet. This was not, nor ever had been, a man out to make trouble. He spent his last moments in prayer speaking in Latin, the language of the Church in whose service he had spent his life. 'Mary, Mother of grace, Mother of mercy, protect us from the enemy, and receive us at the hour of our death.' He was told the hangman was ready, his arms were crossed over his chest and the ladder was kicked from under him. In sentencing, the judge had ordered that Father Garnet 'be cut down alive, and to have his Privy parts cut off and burnt before his Face, as being unworthily begotten, and unfit to leave any Generation after him. His Bowels and inlay'd Parts taken out and burnt . . . After, to have his head cut off, which had imagined the Mischief. And lastly, his Body to be quartered . . .'

Garnet's body danced and just as the hangman was preparing to cut it down a number of the crowd rushed forward and pushed him aside. As they did so others pulled at his legs, an act of mercy often performed by relatives, to make the end swifter. He was dead when the hangman cut him down and using a long-handled butcher's knife proceeded to castrate him, disembowel him – to draw him – and hack him into four joints – to quarter him. No cheering when his heart was held aloft for all to see and no one cried out 'God save the King' as was usual at such moments. Instead the crowd groaned, not because they had never seen anything like this, executions being well attended, but because they knew this to be a good man killed for no good reason.

It is possible to read about this period of history and think that England was a country in the grip of madness. Religion was politics and politics meant power. There had been a conflict – Mr Henry Garnet, born in Lancashire, was a subject of the King but Father Henry Garnet, priest of the Society of Jesus, was a priest answerable to God. This issue – God or King – was played out again and again in the coming years and no one, including those about to step into Saltford's story, was unaffected.

But for all the talk of religion and politics, most people thought that anyone who died for religious convictions did so for no good reason. They were too busy getting on with the stuff of life – growing crops, making money, bringing up children – to be overly concerned with a new translation of the Bible. Perhaps its real achievement was not political, nor even religious in the normal sense of the word, but something altogether different. Generations later, many who have read it would agree with Martin Luther that 'The Bible is alive, it speaks to me; it has feet, it runs after me; it has hands, it lays hold on me.' He might perhaps have added: it has music, it sings to me –

This is my Commaundement, that ye loue one another,
as I haue loued you.
Greater loue hath no man then this, that a man lay downe
his life for his friends.

In the closing decades of the previous century and now, in the
opening of the new one, a lot of lives had been 'laid down' and the
translators, perhaps especially the two who had witnessed Henry
Garnet's gruesome end, hoped that their work would herald a more
moderate age. It was not difficult to see how the tension between
Protestant and Catholic would shape something like a Bible; harder
to see how it would shape a house. It was now, as if prompted by
the arrival of this new Bible with its promise of new beginnings,
that Saltford approached what was to be its most dramatic transformation. In a preview of the divide later to erupt in the Civil War,
this house, for so long the home of landed and titled merchants,
the 'Popish persons' feared by the translators, slid into the hard-
working hands of a family of yeoman farmers, the men and women
defined by the translators as 'self-conceited brethren'.

Lamorock Flower married Ann Brode in 1621 on the porch
outside the doors of St Mary's church; no readings, no singing, no
walking down the aisle. All that came much later. In those days
they simply said vows and declared themselves to be living as man
and wife. Presents were exchanged and the priest kissed Lamorock
who passed this kiss to the bride – the origin of 'You may now kiss
the bride' in our marriage services. And that was it: they were married. Usually the wedding breakfast took place in the groom's
house, which in this case could hardly have been more convenient.
The throng of guests gathered around the couple (the Flowers
were a large family) would carry the bride and groom to the bedroom, empty flagons and laughter trailing in their wake. No
accounts exist of what happened on this day but nothing in the
couple's subsequent history even hints at anything approaching
drunken excess, rather the opposite.

The wedding had taken place outside the very same church doors
where I found myself on the day of Brian's funeral. It transpired

that he had been ill for some time: prostate cancer which spread. The church was full, perhaps a hundred and fifty people. I made my way past the King James Bible, down the aisle and up to the choir stalls. People were still coming, neighbours, friends, nurses who had helped his wife, Joyce, in the last days. I rewound some memories: Brian leaning over the wall while Joyce was arranging church flowers; chatting about roses and lawn fertiliser. The last time I had seen him he had looked so ill, determinedly trying to be cheerful, but now, in my imagination, he seemed effortlessly well, almost younger. Another memory: Sunday morning, Brian at the top of the house, fiddling with his cardigan buttons and thanking me on behalf of the village for agreeing to take the house on. The air was heavy with so much: sadness certainly, but there was something else, difficult to name but impossible to miss.

The words of the ceremony rolled out, but it was the bugle call – the last post, lingering notes and silences – which sounded most clearly. The service probably should have ended there, nothing more to be said. But words will not be defeated so easily and here they had power, coming from some far-off place.

> *The Lord is my shepherd; I shall not want.*
> *He maketh me to lie downe in green pastures;*
> *he leadeth me beside still waters.*

The coffin was carried out shoulder-high. I shuffled silently through the porch, knowing that this book, resident here since 1613, hidden under a black leather shroud in a glass tomb, had spoken to me.

# 9

# Lamorock and Ann

OUR FIRST CHRISTMAS in the country was a lonely affair. It was not that people were unfriendly, rather the opposite. We were asked to parties by families we barely knew; but here, in what was effectively a new country, we felt dislocated, as if struggling with a new language. Even food shopping, never a personal favourite, seemed more than usually difficult this year.

'Can I have four turkey breasts?'

'Just the breasts?' Pause.

'Yes.'

'You mean *breasts*?'

There must have been something odd about the way I asked because the butcher stepped out from behind his counter to supplement his last question with a visual aid. Taking a deep breath he stood on tiptoes, puffed up his chest and used his hands to make his chest more fulsome. It was the kind of small, inconsequential thing that made us wonder if there was something here, some secret code, about which we had not been told.

In fact, the explanation was simple: I was preoccupied with money and builders and Anna, with two children under school age, was missing all the friends we had taken for granted in London. It would not have taken much during the cold dark weeks leading up to Christmas to call the two removal men from *Four Weddings and a Funeral* and ask them to take us back to London. I had lived in London for nearly twenty years but had never, as far as I am aware, spent even one moment thinking about the Regent Street Christmas lights or the Christmas tree hanging from the front of Harrods – until now. If I had been asked about them I would have said they were cheesy and commercial, but sitting in Avon Cottage, wrapping the girls' presents on a cheerless December night, they seemed reassuring, even romantic; the English version of New York film locations where everyone is clutching large, upright brown paper bags stuffed with presents. If we were in a film, it was more like one of those cruel television programmes where the camera follows a family in pursuit of an ideal lifestyle which everyone can see is going to end in ruin. In reality we now owned the shell of a house which was probably worth less than we had paid for it. We could not afford to go back to London.

I recall one particularly bleak evening. It had been one of those cold blue winter days, the sort that look good on a Christmas card. Anna drove around to the house for the daily check to see if there were any builders on site. The garden looked beautiful, flattered by the light snow which had fallen the previous night. She arrived at the gates, stopping just in time to see the trench, which I had forgotten to tell her about, carved right across the garden. After scrambling across the trench, she picked her way across the massive piles of snow-covered earth and arrived at the front door which was swinging in the wind. She looked at the bare stone walls covered by a tangle of wires and pipes, down to what had once been the hall floor but was now a large expanse of compacted sand and gravel. Tightening her grip on the sample book of curtain material she had been studying for the last week, she burst into tears.

That evening, as we sat wrapping more presents, I tried to be cheerful. I told her all about the past, focusing on funny things from Lamorock's time, but when I could see this was not working I tried to create the future, a future full of sunny days with us installed happily in the house. Little did she know that on my way to the public library, to research the past, and the builders' merchants, to build this hoped-for future, I was studying estate agents' windows trying to assess exactly how much we would lose if we had to sell the place.

Bath was full of festive cheer and street stalls selling outsize rolls of wrapping paper. A little group of red-faced men and jolly women dressed in Dickensian costumes were singing carols outside the estate agents' window, panes of glass framed with sprayed-on snow.

*Snow had fallen, snow on snow,*
*Snow on snow,*
*In the bleak mid-winter,*
*Long ago.*

As 1621 drew to a close, Lamorock and Ann were letting the house wrap itself around them, making their first home together in what must have seemed to them a wonderful place to spend the winter months. The time was fast coming when anyone caught celebrating Christmas would be jailed for heresy. Christmas – literally Christ's mass – was heavy with Catholic associations and all good Puritans, and even those not so good, were determined to seek out and remove all practices not commanded in the Bible. A common saying among them was 'Brown bread and the gospel is good fare', good perhaps but so dull. It was impossible to imagine the people who poured themselves so extravagantly into the fabric of this house spending their first Christmas crouching over their Bible and eating rough bread.

Indeed, my picture was rather different: 24 December 1621 – Ann in the kitchen with two or three servants. These women were not hidden away in a separate part of the house, as they would be in later centuries, but allowed to live and work alongside their mistress. They were seldom more than a few metres away from her at any moment in the day. Ann holds a recipe up to the nearest lamp:

Take a Pottle of Cream, and boil in it a little whole
Cinnamon, and three or four flakes of Mace. To this
proportion of Cream put in eighteen yolkes of Eggs, and
eight of the whites; a pint of Sack [sweet wine]. Beat your
Eggs very well, and mingle them with your Sack, Put in three
quarters of a pound of Sugar into the Wine and Eggs with a
Nutmeg grated, and a little beaten Cinnamon; set the basin
on fire with the wine and Eggs, and let it be hot. Then put in
the Cream boyling from the fire, pour it on high, but stir it
not; cover it with a dish, and when it is settled, strew on the
top a little fine Sugar mingled with three grains of
Ambergreece and one grain of Musk and serve it up.

Ann lifts the bowl full of the smooth creamy drink, the texture of thick soup, and pours it into her best pewter jug. Carrying it the short distance across the holly-coated hall into the dining room, I saw her smiling at Lamorock, who was standing to one side of Walter's roaring fireplace, in front of him a table full of guests, wooden platters of cold meats, fine white bread and everywhere laughter.

The Flowers had chosen a dramatic moment to make their first appearance – Roundheads and Cavaliers, the execution of Charles I, maypoles and Milton – but there was little about them to demand centre stage. Unlike the previous principal actors they appeared, seemingly, from nowhere. The archives were silent, no wills, marriage certificates, just the name itself. The *Oxford Dictionary of Surnames* suggests two possible sources:

**Flower 1.** Nickname for flower, blossom. This was a conventional term of endearment in medieval romantic poetry. **2.** Occupational name for a miller or flour merchant, or perhaps a nickname for a pasty-faced person.

I struggled to see Lamorock answering to 'blossom'; easier to see him with a pasty face or as a flour merchant. Lamorock and Ann's story revolved around work. They began as tenants, worked and bought a freehold share in the house, worked harder and embarked on the most ambitious make-over the house had ever known, worked still harder and passed their considerable holding on to the next generation – all this as the clouds of the Civil War continued to gather overhead.

They opened a new chapter in Saltford's story. It was significant that their initials, LF and AF, were at the centre of the two most important rooms, the bedroom and the sitting room. For the first time the people living in the house earned their living from working the land. For farmers, business life and family life often merge, sharing as they do the same location. And so it was that Saltford, always an admired house, a place of standing, now became a place of work and family.

A contemporary, writing about his idealised country girl some six years before Lamorock and Ann were married, may well have described some of the qualities Lamorock saw in his wife. 'All her excellencies stand in her so silently, as if they had stolen upon her without her knowledge. The lining of her apparel (which is herself) is far better than the outsides of tissue; for though she be not arrayed in the spoil of silkworm, she is decked in innocency, a far better wearing.' The idea that inner beauty is a better thing than fine clothes is clearly not a new one. Where Lamorock saw a pretty, fresh-faced lover, his parents might well have seen a suitable wife for their son and mother for their grandchildren. Perhaps they saw in Ann 'the virtues which ought to be in a complete woman, as her skill in physic, cookery, banqueting-stuff, distillation, perfumes, wool, hemp, flax, dairies, brewing, baking and all other things belonging to a household'. In the event both were right; the innocent girl turned into the complete wife.

It would have been surprising if Lamorock and Ann's first winter in their new home, surrounded by family and friends, was not a happy one. For the out-of-work labourers who drifted around the villages hoping to pick up casual work in the fields, life was very different. The wool industry, on which the Rodney wealth had been based and on which many more modest livings had depended, was collapsing and the harvest had been poor. In the event a run of bad weather over the next few years caused repeated harvests to fail. But what was hard for some – too many people chasing too little work – was good for others, and the Flowers with their ambition and their newly acquired 112 acres of land were on the right side of the equation. Remarkably, considering the general state of the economy and the size of this new family, they managed, in 1627, to purchase a one-third share in the freehold of Saltford Manor.

Ann, some six years into married life, was a busy woman. She rose just before sunrise, ate breakfast, a selection of cold meats, bread and butter and ale, and then set to work. In the early years, when she and Lamorock were making their way, she would have spent hours churning butter in the dairy or roasting barley in the brewery. Water often made people sick and milk was only suitable for the very young or very old; the alternative was to drink beer. Ann had watched her parents brewing beer and now she herself was surrounded by smells she had known all her life, stirring buckets of roasted barley into hop-flavoured boiling water. She used the malted barley three times; the first brew made very strong beer, which because of the hops could be kept for two years. This was followed by a second and then a third much weaker brew, known as small beer, which everyone drank when they were thirsty. Eight pints a day was not unusual.

There is a nursery rhyme said to have been written around this time about Cherrington Manor in Shropshire, but it could as well have been about Saltford Manor.

> *This is the farmer sowing the corn,*
> *That kept the cock that crowed in the morn,*
> *That waked the priest all shaven and shorn,*
> *That married the man all tattered and torn,*
> *That kissed the maiden all forlorn,*
> *That milked the cow with the crumpled horn,*
> *That tossed the dog,*
> *That killed the rat,*
> *That ate the malt*
> *That lay in the house that Jack built.*

Exactly *where* the malt lay probably did not matter very much, certainly not to the rats who were eating it. In any event Ann's primary responsibility was the preparation of food for the human beings in her household, and in an age where there was no running water or fridges, and when the only source of heat was wood or coal fires, preparing meals was hard work.

Fashionable society in London had begun to experiment with Continental dishes like Italian macaroni and Spanish olla-podrida, an amazing variety of stewed meats and vegetables, brought down to earth and Anglicised as 'hotch-potch'. But Saltford was a long way from London, in every sense, and the Flowers had no time for the ever-increasing range of recipe books, which between 1600 and 1700 appeared almost every other year. Country people were suspicious of highly priced Frenchified 'Hogg-podg Dish-meats' cooked 'A-la-Mode' and covered in suspicious-looking 'A-la-Sauces'. Lamorock liked plain, wholesomely cooked roasts and he liked bread. The 'great cakes' of Walter's time, enriched with butter, cream, eggs and sugar, heavily fruited and spiced and weighing more than 9 kilos, were often to be smelt in Ann's kitchen. The poet George Herbert was right, 'Of all smells, bread; of all tastes, salt', and Ann's kitchen had plenty of both. The need to preserve whatever was in season against the time when it was not, was a feature of her life. Salting, the rubbing of large quantities of course rough salt into meat, was not a pleasant task. Ann's hands were red and chapped, cuts and grazes open to what must have been the near-daily sting of salt.

And then there was the washing: one of the most physical of domestic duties. It is likely that Ann employed a washerwoman to help her with this task that might well have taken at least two days a week. The water was drawn from a well in the garden, which meant that most of the washing took place in a large wooden tub outdoors. The garments, shirts, sheets, table clothes were placed in the tub with sticks between each layer of linen to allow the water to pass through easily, and then soaked in a strong alkaline solution called 'ley', the seventeenth-century version of washing powder. Once the dirt had been loosened the linen was rinsed in clean water. None of this was easy, but it was as nothing compared with the next stage. Linen, when first produced, is a grey-cream colour and the fashion of the time, much like today, preferred white to off-white or grey-white or too-many-washes white. The easiest, cheapest source of ammonia was human urine, so . . . Ann's washerwoman would have argued strongly in favour of lime, only just being used as a bleaching agent.

Dinner, consisting of two courses, was the main meal of the day and taken at midday. Each course was a meal in itself, including both sweets and savouries, rather like a modern buffet. The family ate in the dining room and the servants sat on stools around the hearth in the kitchen. In the early years both family and servants ate from the light-biscuit-coloured platters that had just begun to be produced at Brislington, midway between Saltford and Bristol, but pewter and even silver were on their way. Forks had been introduced in London but it would be another thirty years before they would be in common use at Saltford. As soon as the meal was finished there was more work to do in the form of sewing, mending and making candles. And then, just as the sun was dipping, all the clothes and sheets that had been left in the garden to bleach had to be brought in so that no hooker with his long pole could lift them over the hedge.

At some point in her early married life Ann became pregnant. In common with all pregnant women at the time, Ann would have been counselled to avoid ugly sights and pictures as it was generally accepted that sudden frights could harm the baby. Today we regard childbirth as a medical event, a time to have skilled doctors and nurses at hand, but for Ann it would have been much more of a social occasion, a time to be near her female friends and relatives. The rituals were centred on giving her female support, and on allowing her to drop out of her normal routine for as long as Lamorock could manage and as long as her health demanded.

The first part of the confinement was called 'taking your chamber'. This meant retiring for about six weeks before the birth to a specially prepared room, perhaps the new room above the kitchen, hung with all the best tapestries. It is perfectly possible that she borrowed some tapestries from her family, the better to decorate her chamber. The windows were tightly closed in order to keep out the harmful fresh air. When labour began, the various friends and family who had already been invited to visit were sent for, along with the midwife. The women were company for Ann and also helped the midwife, making up fortifying drinks to keep up her strength and her spirits.

It is impossible to say how many women or children died in childbirth – but certainly enough for everyone to know someone who had. Indeed, considering the public nature of the event, many women must have watched a relative or friend die in the agony of childbirth. A woman writing to her pregnant friend in 1623 said, 'Itt trobels me more to hear how apprehensive you are of a danger itt hath pleased God to carry you so often safely through' – the woman to whom the letter was written had been 'carried through' three times already and this was to be her fourth pregnancy. Nevertheless she was frightened and with good reason; if anything did go wrong there was little the midwife could do. Today natural birth is one of a range of options; in those days it was all there was.

Baby Lamorock (the boy was named after his father) was washed and swaddled, which involved wrapping him in linen bands from head to toe to prevent him growing up with a physical deformity. After a month his arms were freed from the swaddling and Ann began to carry him about, but it was not until he was about eight or nine months old that the swaddling was completely abandoned. She must have been tempted not to change him as often as necessary; wrapping and unwrapping layers of swaddling bands is a long way from Mothercare disposable nappies.

As for Ann, she was kept in bed in a darkened room for the first three days; labour was thought to weaken the eyesight. After this it was time for her 'upsitting', which was essentially a social occasion to which her friends were invited back for a meal. After the ceremony there was a further week or so when Ann was allowed out of bed but still confined to her chamber. Finally, after several weeks, Ann was allowed to walk around the house but not out of doors.

By 1637 Lamorock and Ann had lived at Saltford for sixteen years and, in common with so many of us, they may well have felt they did not want to leave. He and Ann knew how to live, they ate and entertained freely, but they were not careless. The precision of what they left – the finely carved mantelpiece and new front façade – did not happen by accident, they were the products of detailed planning. In the early part of the seventeenth century the process of building was changing. In Walter Rodney's time a rough plan had been devised which was modified as work progressed. The detailing, like the stone and wooden mantelpiece, was done by the craftsmen concerned, the master mason and master carpenter. John Rodney's builders, with their robes and efficiency, had brought new levels of organisation to the building process but now, some fifty years later, buildings were being shaped by architects, men like Inigo Jones who was transforming London. The materials were shaped to the idea rather than the other way around, and the idea that appears to have informed Saltford's architect was simple: light.

In the spring, Lamorock's builders began work on what was to be the most radical transformation of the house. Saltford was to be turned around, no longer to face the fields as it had done since Domesday. It has been said that windows are the eyes of a house; if this is so then Lamorock gave Saltford great eyesight. The seven mullioned windows are positioned across the southern face of the house exactly as they should be. Walk up the drive and see the house for the first time and most people feel they have seen it before; they have, in countless photos of country houses built in the seventeenth century. He also gave it an elm-lined timber staircase laid over Walter's stone steps, a massive new loft for the servants to sleep in and, best of all, a high-mantled stone fireplace in the principal bedroom. The stone for this mantelpiece probably came from the quarry at Combe Down, a five-mile journey on a specially strengthened wagon.

Sitting on the wagon was Lamorock's master mason, the most important man on the site, and a carter. Here, on the top of the wide spaces of rolling green, the two men sat, probably in silence. No need to talk, nothing to say. Over to the west, on the Chiltern Hills, the sun picked out the huge white chalk horse. Eventually the cart announced itself by rattling and grinding its way across the gravel which led down towards the quarry.

The stones, which had been blasted out of the open rock face by gunpowder, had been cut into manageable blocks, levered onto customised logs and rolled into the workshop. The mason selected what was needed for the bedroom mantelpiece, chalking what amounted to full-size working drawings on the workshop floor. The stone-sawyers, whose job it was to cut the stone, watched intently as the mason, on his hands and knees, parchment held flat by pieces of stone, chalked out the exact dimensions.

The result was spectacular. Lamorock's initials were set off to the side of Ann's on the lip of this beautifully crafted fireplace. The carving was finely done, initials and date set within a shallow indentation to help them stand out, the numbers 6, 3 and 7 all slightly lopsided, skewed off to the right as if squashed from above. The fireplace graced a room which held Lamorock and Ann's most prized piece of furniture: a bed with a mattress laid on strips of canvas mesh rather than boards. Beds such as these were so valuable and durable that they were left in wills and passed down from father to son. In nearly all homes the bed was the most important piece of furniture – it was certainly the most comfortable. Ann had taken special care to save feathers plucked from her poultry for the mattresses and pillows. Also in the room was a stool and a cupboard for jugs and basins, brushes and combs, a looking-glass and, rather more practically, a chamberpot enclosed in a stool covered with leather or cloth. These were known as 'close-stools' or 'necessary-stools' until the Victorians, with their distaste for the body, decided to call them night commodes.

In the aftermath of the building work, which must have taken its toll on Lamorock and Ann, just as it was doing on us, people would have flowed in and out of the house every day. The physical division between home and work was not clearly defined as it is today: Saltford would have been effectively the head office of what was fast becoming a prosperous family business. Ann would occasionally retreat up to her new private bedchamber. The woman I imagined lay on the fine counterpane that covered her bed, took long deep breaths and looked up at the ceiling – a network of woodwork and plaster like a beautifully ridged timber fan. The bed itself was covered by a colourful silk tapestry hung from the ceiling by hooks, three of which are still evident today. Sometimes, during a rare moment of quiet, Lamorock might have crept upstairs and sat on the edge of the bed. Perhaps they spoke of Robert, the son they had lost some years earlier, or of what their parents would have said – if they had lived – to see them living in such style.

They were, although they could not have known it at the time, in the autumn of their marriage. This practical man had set his wife's initials centre frame in this, the showpiece of his newly transformed home. How he felt about the future is a matter for conjecture; no letters or diaries remain since he was not the writing type. But he was a loving man and might well have agreed with these lines written just after the turn of the century: 'Is not old wine wholesomest, old pippins [apples] toothsomest, old wood burns brightest, old linen washest whitest? Old soldiers, sweetheart, are surest, and old lovers are soundest.'

Lamorock died two years later on 6 April 1639. He was 38, hardly old by our standards and not even by theirs. In the nave of St Mary's is a memorial to Lamorock, commissioned by Ann in the weeks following his death. The mason started well enough, cutting the following into the centre of the stone:

HEARE LYETH
THE BODY OF
LAMOROCK FLOWER
WHO DECEASEDTHE
6 DAY OF APRIL 1639
FLOWERS THEY WAR
NIPT IN Y SPRINGE
BUT FLOURISHING NOW
WITH CHRIST THEIR KING

Cutting around the rim like an inscription around a plate, he had begun in the top left-hand corner with another name: ROBERT FLOWER. Robert, almost certainly the son Ann and Lamorock had lost some eight years earlier, now crowned the tablet and all was set fair. Full of hope, he continued: WHO DECEASED. By now he was at the bottom right-hand corner with more words to cut. Chisel in hand, he might have paused for a moment to weigh his options: turn the stone upside down or, and this was his master-stroke, spell the remaining words backwards and hope that not too many people would notice. The bottom line reads: YAD 51 EHT; on reaching the bottom right-hand corner he breathed a sigh of relief and continued more conventionally: OF JULY 1631.

I searched for some sign of Ann but could find nothing. I wondered how long she lived after Lamorock and what became of her relationship with her eldest son and her son's wife. Lamorock's memorial was touching, almost because it was so bodged, and it said something about Ann's low regard for appearance. Another woman would have thrown it away and employed the mason who had done their bedroom carving. Ann was what Shakespeare called a 'queen of curds and cream' and it seemed wrong that in this place dedicated to memory there was a memorial to her husband and son but nothing of her, and then . . .

As I walked across the fields to Avon Cottage, a new thought came to mind, dropped, it seemed on that late February afternoon, from on high. Life was about as close to death as Lamorock and Ann's bedroom was to the churchyard – a matter of perhaps 25 metres – and yet, amazingly, this realisation was uplifting, even joyous. An American writer put it well:

> *send me out into another life*
> *lord because this one is growing faint*
> *I do not think it goes all the way*

Some time later I saw Joyce at the bottom of the drive, unloading some flowers from the back of her car.

'Hi Joyce.'

'Oh hello.'

'How are you doing?'

'Oh . . .' she shrugged and smiled, 'you know.'

'No, but I can guess.'

'Some days are not bad and others . . .' Her mouth tightened and she waved her hand from side to side, like a ship on some waves.

'Which is it today?'

'Oh.' More hand movements. 'It's difficult' – she gestured to the flowers she was going to put next to Brian's ashes – 'coming here with these.'

'Of course.'

'People have been so kind, I'm always being asked out but . . . well you know.' She looked sad and brave. And then, after a moment, she continued, 'I know it sounds funny but he's the lucky one, isn't he?'

# · 10 ·

# Pride and Plaster

1640: SALTFORD with its new eyes and face looked out on one of the most dramatic decades in English history. Within ten years the King of England had been executed and there followed a series of events which even today seems incredible. A republic was established, communes spread across Surrey (of all places!), the House of Lords was abolished, established religion was blown apart and last, perhaps most shockingly, the grand finale to this extraordinary sequence: a military dictatorship was established. And all on English soil.

This was England's revolution, a time of radical ideas which sprang, to a large degree, from the lower and middling sorts: the yeoman farmers and small tradesmen, men who had previously had no place at the tables of power. When one yeoman farmer was commissioning the overhaul of a little-known manor house in Somerset, another was tilling the land in East Anglia. The East Anglian yeoman was called Oliver Cromwell. He was to become *the* figure of the next twenty years, striding across the political landscape of his time like a colossus. He dismissed Parliament some four years after the King's death with these words: 'You have sat too long here for any good you have been doing. Depart, I say, and let us have done with you. In the name of God, go!' The same words were spoken by the Tory MP Leo Amery to urge Neville Chamberlain to resign in 1940. Today, statues of both Cromwell and Winston Churchill sit outside the Houses of Parliament. Churchill, shoulders hunched, hands in the pockets of his greatcoat, scowls defiantly, and Cromwell, sitting astride his horse, looks off to the horizon, head held high. Both men combined a genius for rhetoric with the common touch; the ability to capture the hearts of men like Lamorock Flower.

In 1640 the Civil War – a series of violent clashes between King and Parliament – was set to rip across the countryside and no area was more closely contested than the West Country. As the war progressed, both armies, as many as 30,000 soldiers, marched from London and Oxford, sweeping through Saltford on their way to Bristol and the South-West. These men needed supplies, food and lodging, and the surrounding countryside became storehouse, granary and barracks. Saltford had been taking a rest, gently meandering through some domestic scenes, but now the holly in the hall and the babies in swaddling bands were replaced by looting armies ravaging crops and homes. The cast was familiar but the names had changed. The Catholics appeared as 'Cavaliers': swashbuckling romance and fine clothes; and the Protestants, or Puritans as they had become, appeared as 'Roundheads', severe haircuts and plain clothes. It was at this point, the stage set for one of the defining conflicts in English history, that, on 2 April 1640, something happened in Saltford. One of the new breed of Puritans, a man called Henry Stork, became the minister of St Mary's church and the village joined the network of Puritan parishes that controlled northern Somerset. It was a significant moment in Saltford's story and one which, true to form, mirrored precisely what was happening in many parts of the country.

Meanwhile, back in London, Henry's fellow preachers inflamed crowds of bullet-headed apprentices who swarmed threateningly around Westminster and Whitehall. The talk in the taverns was passionate but lacked imagination: rumours of a Spanish invasion and plots to blow up Parliament, reruns of old plotlines. Suspected Catholics and courtiers were assaulted in the street. Once again London had become a dangerous place. By the summer of 1642 the lines had been drawn, both King and Parliament demanded loyalty; it was decision time. The commander of Parliament's western army wrote to his old friend, the commander of the King's western army: 'That great God, which is the searcher of my heart, knows with what a sad sense I go upon this service and with what perfect hatred I detest this war without an enemy. We are both upon this stage and must act those parts that are assigned to us in this tragedy.' The part assigned to Lamorock junior was modest, bordering on invisible. It might have been completely invisible were it not for a piece of paper held in the National Records Office.

> A Note of the names of Such as Sett forth Horses with their furniture, and men with Armes and monney under the Command of Col. Alexander Popham

There followed a list of contributors: Nathaniel Saunders, Tho Pope, Thomas Shephearde, Mr Wm Buckle, Thomas Leman and then:

> Mr Flower One horse and
> the Armes & other attormadations for the same    8   0   0
> and to him that roade the Horse      18   0

Lamorock, as one of the 'people of ability', had been asked for a voluntary contribution by the local parliamentary committee and had given a horse and riding equipment worth £8 and 18 shillings towards the wages of the rider. Of the 28 people who contributed from Keynsham, Saltford and the surrounding countryside, no one contributed more.

As historical discoveries go, this was hardly groundbreaking. Nevertheless, this unremarkable entry on a piece of parchment, little more than a receipt issued by a nameless official listing gifts long since forgotten by people no one ever heard of again, felt important. Once again it was the fact that these were forgotten faceless people, just names on a list, combined with the bread-and-butter nature of their gifts that moved me. Lamorock gave a horse, others gave muskets, swords, plate and donations of between five and ten shillings.

Proper history is all about coronations and thrones, heavily framed portraits and weighty Acts of Parliament; Saltford's history is all about bedrooms and windows, initials on fireplaces and gifts of horses. The events of most of our lives never reach the pages of history – we never do anything sufficiently important, never think big thoughts and therefore do not leave much of ourselves behind when we die. The Flowers were no different, but they did leave something. They left their home. They turned Saltford around to face the sun and they did so using a variety of limestone called Blue Lias. It is this stone, softly mottled with golden-green lichens, which gives the house its classic country frontage. It seems to soak up the sunshine, making its rich surface more beautiful than the page of any document. But now, unusually for Saltford, stone and paper came together – no literary work, no classical architecture, but a receipt for the gift of a horse and a protruding stone to the left of the front door. This stone, a half-pace above ground level, slightly proud of the rest of the elevation, had been used for mounting Lamorock's horses, one of which had been given to Colonel Popham.

This much was clear: Lamorock supported Parliament. Oliver Cromwell, who began the war as a Captain of Horse in Parliament's eastern army, writing about recruiting 'godly honest men' said, 'I had rather have a plain russet-coated captain what knows what he fights for, and loves what he knows, than that which you call a gentleman and is nothing else.' On the evidence of Lamorock's contribution, given some weeks before the outbreak of hostilities, Lamorock Flower was, at the very least, a supporter of such men.

A month before the King declared war on Parliament, representatives of both sides, eager to establish a foothold in the region they considered to hold the key to future success, converged on Bath. Words were spoken and the Royalists, realising they were outnumbered, withdrew to set up their headquarters in Wells. Meanwhile the local Parliamentary leaders, who included Col. Alexander Popham, the man to whom Lamorock had given his horse, called on their supporters. On the night of 5 August, some two weeks before the war proper had started, Colonel Popham's newly equipped Bath Regiment joined a vast crowd of 12,000 who were preparing to spend the night sleeping rough on the hills overlooking the ancient cathedral. Such a huge gathering was remarkable; the entire population of Bristol, the country's largest port and second-largest city, was 15,000.

The meeting, closer to an open-air religious convention than the rendezvous of an army, was a passionate affair. The night passed in fasting and prayer. The small Royalist contingent holed up in Wells, originally some 900 men, shrank still further during the night as many ran up the hill to join friends in the other camp.

As dawn broke, cartloads of provisions, supplied by sympathetic nearby villagers, trundled along the rolling hilltops towards this makeshift camp. After a hearty breakfast Popham's men, joined by local villagers armed with 'pitchforks, dung picks and suchlike weapons, not knowing who they were to fight but supposing they were papists', swept headlong down the hill. They stormed into the cathedral where they began a riot of destruction, smashing the precious stained-glass windows, destroying the organ and altar and trashing the bishop's palace. According to an eyewitness, a portrait of the Virgin Mary was 'put on a spear and carried about in contempt and derision'.

The previous night, those sitting around a roaring campfire may have included the Saltford troop. If Lamorock was amongst them, and as their patron it is possible that he was, he may have seen some of the soldiers smashing the butts of their muskets through windows and altar rails. If these men, sick with a kind of madness, were to ransack Saltford, all that his father had worked for and possibly even the physical safety of his own mother would be at risk. Across the country, grander, more prestigious houses would indeed be ruined: carvings hacked, paintings scrubbed, destroyed by the spirit of the time.

Before the Civil War was over, nearly a quarter of a million people would die, a higher proportion of the population than in any war until the Great War. The opposing armies tracked and retracked up and down the corridor of northern Somerset leaving trails of carnage. In 1644, after two years of some of the bloodiest fighting these islands had seen, a moderate Parliamentarian made a speech to the House of Commons.

> Whose houses are burnt? Whose limbs are cut or shorn off? Whose persons are thrown into loathsome dungeons? Whose blood stains the walls of our towns and defiles our land? Is not all English? . . . I know, sir, you are all here of the same opinion with me in this point; and that it was an unhappy mistake of those who told us in the beginning of our warfare, that it would only be to show ourselves in the field with a few forces, and then all would be presently ended. We have found it otherwise.

So had the people of Saltford. There appeared across all the counties of the West what was arguably the greatest popular movement of the entire war – a string of regionally based self-defence bands, called 'clubmen', drawn primarily from the lower orders of society: the yeoman farmers like Lamorock; the peasantry like Lamorock's tenants; and the clergy like Henry Stork. One of the leaders, possibly Lamorock, arranged for a watch to be maintained and for the church bells to be rung whenever groups of rampaging soldiers were spotted. All the able-bodied men were expected to rush to assemble on the village green, the area at the bottom of our drive and next to the village hall, whenever the signal was given.

But there was another, perhaps more significant, wave of chaos breaking upon the country. With the abolition of the bishops, the structure of the Church of England, the official state-approved Church for the last one hundred years, began to collapse. Christmas was declared illegal, because according to an Act passed by Parliament it gave 'liberty to carnall and sensual delights'. Fanaticism, hardly a classic English quality, was everywhere and new, radical groupings appeared almost daily. There were the Diggers (who began digging up swathes of Surrey in order to turn the earth into a common treasury), the Quakers (who shook or quaked under the power of the Holy Spirit), the Fifth Monarchists (who were anticipating the arrival of the monarchy of Christ), and the Ranters (known for their visions and rampant promiscuity). Behind them were about twenty sorts of Anabaptists, fourteen following Alstedius and the rest following Bullinger, different sorts of Familists, Brownists, Donatistical Brownists, Antinomians, Arminians, Sabbatarians and Anti-Sabbatarians, Traskites and Hetheringtonians. By the mid-1640s there were thirty to forty separate congregations in London.

Religion was hot news, pamphlets and broadsheets flooded onto the streets of London, some condemning the new groupings as rebels against God and others publicising what they saw as new, exciting forms of worship. On the title page of one of the most famous, fish were in the sky, wheelbarrows pushed men, horses stood up on their hind legs pushing wagons and the church was upside down.

I recalled a moment from one of Chris the Curate's videos, this one snappily titled 'What about the Church?' The only thing that was upside down in the village hall that night was the course manual owned by an elderly gentleman from Keynsham who had nodded off and allowed his booklet to slide face-down on the floor. As I looked around the half-dozen people I now vaguely knew, the only people in the village remotely interested in the subject, no one was digging up their gardens, there was not much shaking under the power of the Holy Spirit, few of us would have called ourselves visionaries, and there was, I felt fairly confident, little rampant promiscuity. The same polo-shirted presenter who had spent the preceding weeks engagingly weaving his way through the Bible was in full flow.

> I was walking across a bridge one day, and I saw a man standing on the edge, about to jump. I ran over and said: 'Stop. Don't do it.'
>
> 'Why shouldn't I?' he asked.
>
> 'Well, there's so much to live for!'
>
> 'Like what?'
>
> 'Are you religious?'
>
> 'Yes.'
>
> 'Me too. Are you Christian or Buddhist?'
>
> 'Christian.'
>
> 'Me too. Are you Catholic or Protestant?'
>
> 'Protestant.'
>
> 'Me too. Are you Episcopalian or Baptist?'
>
> 'Baptist.'
>
> 'Wow. Me too. Are you Baptist Church of God or Baptist Church of the Lord?'
>
> 'Baptist Church of God.'
>
> 'Me too. Are you original Baptist Church of God, or are you reformed Baptist Church of God?'
>
> 'Reformed Baptist Church of God.'
>
> 'Me too. Are you Reformed Baptist Church of God, reformation of 1879, or Reformed Baptist Church of God, reformation of 1915?'

He said: 'Reformed Baptist Church of God, reformation of 1915.'

I said: 'Die, heretic scum,' and pushed him off.

In the mid-seventeenth century there were plenty of people ready to push others off bridges but Lamorock was not one of them. By 1645 most people had had enough of war, wanting to get on with their lives, which is exactly what Lamorock appears to have done because in that year he married a local landowner's daughter, Elizabeth Goodhind. To say that the house tells this chapter of the story would be an exaggeration, but it hints at it.

The plaster panel above Walter's oak mantelpiece had intrigued me on our first trip around the house and continued to do so. It flew majestically above Walter's fireplace, initials and dates embedded in two shields surrounded by ornate frames, angel wings, scrolls – a sort of relaxed family flag. Lamorock's initials were joined with those of his new wife on the left-hand shield and 1645, the date of their marriage, was on the right-hand shield. But the centre, the place of honour, was reserved for the woman around whom Saltford, his childhood home, had revolved – his mother Ann. How much better that Ann's memorial should be here, in one of the warmest parts of the house, rather than on a cold green stone in St Mary's graveyard.

The plasterwork looks like something one of the great families of the land might place between two suits of armour in a prominent place in the family seat; the current residents were farmers on the make, who until a few years ago could only afford to rent. In addition to this, the war was in the process of ruining many but it did not, judging from this plaster panel, ruin the Flowers. As a Devonshire yeoman said of another yeoman and his wife, 'When this John and Mary were first married, they had but little, but God did so prosper them that before she died they had 400 bullocks and a great store of money and other such stuff and were as well furnished of all things in their house as any one man of their degree in all the country.' When Lamorock and Ann had first married they hadn't had much either but somehow they had managed to leave their son with enough money 'and other such stuff' to pay for further improvements to the house. Lamorock junior had backed what was to be the winning side and it is perfectly possible that he might, as a flour merchant, have actually increased his wealth during the first three years of war.

Nevertheless, yeoman farmers usually preferred to spend their hard-earned money expanding their land base rather than paying for coats of arms. But at Saltford it seems no one, not even a family of down-to-earth farmers, was ever entirely safe from the odd moment of weakness. The Flowers clearly aspired to some heraldry, but aspirations here are not quite the same as elsewhere. Lamorock's plaster panel is charming because it is so transparently *not* the real thing. It is modest, consisting as it does of shapes which must, judging from their irregularities, have been modelled freehand with the fingers, aided by a few small tools and perhaps a beeswax mould. This is the homespun heraldry of a newly married man who wanted, like his father before him, to leave his mark on a house he loved.

The man who built this panel was a local man, a world away from those used by Sir Roger Pratt, one of the great English architects of the time, who advised all engaged in house-building to 'get some ingenious gentlemen, who had seen much of this kind of thing abroad and been somewhat versed in the best authors of architecture viz. Palladio, Scamozzi, Serlio etc. to do it for you, and to give you a design of it on paper – which will generally fall out better than one by a home-bred architect for want of his better experience as is daily seen'. Italian, according to Sir Roger, was good, English was ordinary. How wrong he was. As an example of seventeenth-century artistry Lamorock's lowly plaster panel was not culturally significant (for a start it was English not Italian), more Smith than Scamozzi, but as an expression of the love that once flowed between a son, his mother and his new wife, it is wonderful. Looking at it as an architectural feature was one thing; sitting in front of it on a winter's night, glass of wine in hand, was quite another.

But wine and love had little to do with plastering walls and I had plenty of those, desperately in need of work. If the eyes of a house are the windows, the bones are the walls and Saltford's bones needed covering. Bare stone has a raw, magnificent simplicity but bare stone covered with a tangle of cables and pipes looks plain ugly. The time had come for us to begin plastering and Mark was the man for the job.

Mark was in his late twenties, with close-cut fair hair and a ready, open face. I liked him immediately. He was tall, broad-shouldered, loose-limbed and went by the surprising name of 'Tweet'. I tried it a few times but ended up sticking to Mark.

We set off up to the bridge, the large room at the top of the house, and immediately, and inevitably, began discussing money. The issue, when it comes to money, is day rate or job rate? In other words, do you pay an agreed figure per day worked or a fixed price for a specific job? Mark said he would prefer a day rate because it promised a better price for what he rightly thought would be a long time. Unsure of which route to take, I phoned Simon the Surveyor, who said that with the building trade there is no such thing as a bargain.

Interestingly Sir Roger, writing some 350 years earlier, shared Simon's cynicism about builders. 'If workmen be employed by the day, they will make small haste to finish the building. If agreed with all by the great as to all particulars . . . the difficulty is very much in making the bargain, which they will be trying to break either in the matter or manner of their working.' The answer, he maintained, was in the supervision of the work, exactly what Simon was saying to me. Sir Roger went on, 'To determine anything without due meditation, is rashness. Not to come to any determination in a convenient time, is an effect of ignorance or sloth.' In other words, if you are supervising the work, will you, as an unqualified person, know if it is any good?

Simon, too polite to call me ignorant or slothful, had said the same. But in the end it was Sir Roger who made my mind up. 'When in doubt,' he said, summarising the professional's approach to buildings, 'we should not trust in the bare force of our imagination.' Enough was enough, I *had* to trust in the 'bare force of my imagination', it was all I had. I called Mark and told him that I felt he seemed to understand the place, a comment which was met by silence, and went on to say that I would like him to start as soon as possible. I agreed to pay a day rate until the house was finished. He stayed for six months, plastering every single wall.

In one sense, plastering is a straightforward job, not unlike buttering a piece of rough cold toast, but these walls were nothing like toast and they were anything but straight; not a right angle in the place. They were all curves and angles, hidden recesses, everything tilting and leaning – a dream to look at but a nightmare to plaster. Set squares and plumb lines, the tools used in standard plastering work, would have destroyed their charm. The only way to properly cover them was to follow their natural contours, which meant looking really closely at each surface, making what amounted to hundreds of small decisions each day. There is something fascinating about watching a skilled man work, the more so if he cannot see you watching. I would find a space in another room, open the door and pretend to look through floor plans. Of all the trades this was the most graceful: slow, quick, quick, slow. Slowly looking, assessing each curve and irregularity, quickly spreading each trowel of the soft pink material across the wall or ceiling in question. The foundation coat was covered by a skim coat: fine easy-to-spread pink butter which he swept across the textured foundation and then, with astonishing lightness of touch, sponged to a glazed pink sheen. The process is dirty and physical. The floor of a room being plastered looks like a dirty pink farmyard, but the effect, or at least the effect of Mark's work, was that of a picture framer preparing work for a gallery. Good framing, like good plastering, does not attract attention to itself, rather it helps the eye to focus on the subject. Alone in the house at the end of a day, we would chat.

'I really love what you are doing. Thanks.'

'Right.'

'No really I mean it . . . I think it's amazing.'

'It's what I do. I've worked on some nice places but nothing with this character. Georgian town houses don't touch this place – all those tall windows, fancy ceilings and straight lines – boring.'

'I agree – I love this place. If it wasn't for the money side it would be paradise.'

'How do you mean?'

'To be honest with you – I really don't know if we've got enough money.'

'Oh I see . . . what if you haven't?'

'I dunno – I guess we'll just have to stop.'

'It'll be all right.'

'Why do you think that?'

'Dunno – just got a feeling. I tell you something – you're a lucky man.'

'I know.'

'Yeah and that's another thing – you talk to us.'

'How do you mean?'

'Well, normally the guy with the money, the main man, reckons himself.'

'I see.'

'But you're . . . I dunno . . . you're like us.' And then, just as it was dawning on me that this was one of the nicest things anyone had said to me in ages, he continued. 'Well – not completely.' We laughed.

One Saturday afternoon Mark arrived at the house with a friend, saying, not altogether convincingly, that he was just passing and needed to pick up some tools for a weekend job he was doing. Would I mind if he showed Nick around? They set off upstairs to the room which he had completed the previous day, the bedroom with the window around which he had spent hours feathering the plaster. I continued to work on my plans, this time quite genuinely, double-checking next week's lighting plot. Sound travels well in empty houses and because we were the only people in the house, I caught snatches of their conversation.

'That's the old window.'

'It's a proper job.'

'See what I mean?'

'Mm.'

No gushing superlatives, nothing about the history, not an adjective in sight . . . and yet, I heard something else behind Mark's words.

Some weeks later a piece of skirting came away by accident and I saw it, scratched into what had recently been wet plaster. 'Tweet was here – 1998'. There it was again – something personal, so easily missed – so Saltford.

# 11

# The Jack Pudding Judge

O N THE WALLS of an elegantly furnished 1970s block of flats in Weybridge, Surrey, sits a small frame containing a fragment of parchment, a little scrap of Saltford.

Alexander Flower was born in 1867, the year before Disraeli became Prime Minister, and lived at Saltford before moving away to get married. He died in 1928, when his daughter June was seven years old, and was buried together with three and a half centuries of assorted Lamorocks in St Mary's churchyard. June, now eighty-six and living in Weybridge, had written to me asking if she could drop in and look around the house on her next visit to her father's grave. In those early months hardly a week went by without someone wandering up the drive and asking if they could look around. But this was more than a casual visit; she had persuaded a couple of friends to bring her up from Surrey, a round trip of some 300 miles, to walk around a house she herself had never lived in. Chatting in the kitchen after a slow amble around the rooms, she spoke freely.

'As a little girl I had a dream; that I was growing something in a garden that I was very pleased with. In the dream, which I had many times, I walked from the garden through a gate in a wall into a churchyard. When I first saw Saltford many years later [this was not her first visit] I realised that this was the garden I had seen in my dream but was puzzled that the gate in the wall looked nothing like the one that now goes into the churchyard. I remember chatting to a man, I think he was the Vicar, who told me the door had been replaced in Victorian times . . . it's difficult to describe and to be honest I'm not sure I understand. I just feel extremely attached to the place, as if I am a part of it. Funny.'

It would have been easy to make sense of all this if June had grown up at Saltford herself, but this had not been the case. The first time she had ever been here was as an adult in her late twenties. Perhaps her father had been fond of talking about the place and she had soaked up all these stories, which after her father's death came seeping out in her dreams: childhood pictures of a place for ever associated with her lost father. The trouble with this theory is that it completely defies the facts. According to June's mother, her husband seldom spoke about Saltford; he had long since left the place. Alexander Flower was an active officer in the British army with little or no desire to dwell on the past.

Strolling around the garden, through the doorway into the churchyard (always one of my favourite places), it occurred to me there may be two different sorts of histories: one written and read, and the other felt and heard. While I had no memory of recurring dreams, and certainly could not say I had ever 'seen' any part of the house before, I had, from the first, felt unusually attracted to this little patch of land, something to do with the huge Scots pine trees in the churchyard, how the house sits on the land . . . I don't honestly know what it was, perhaps the anticipation of adventure, of bridging two worlds, the past and the present.

Sir Walter Raleigh, the Elizabethan adventurer who made a name for himself by laying his cloak in a puddle for his Queen, is said to have given up writing his *History of the World* when he looked out of his window and saw two men arguing. Try as he might, he simply could not work out what it was they were arguing about; he could not hear them, could only try to guess at the reason for their argument by reading their body language. In that moment he decided to abandon his writing, concluding that no one can ever establish the complete truth about anything. June's visit had the opposite effect on me. It confirmed what I had always felt: that I was never going to know the whole truth about Saltford. That, it had always seemed to me, was the joy of the place, which is not to say that the bits that are knowable, like the framed parchment which she had brought for me to see, were not precious.

This tax receipt, a throwaway object to the people of the time, together with two silver plates engraved with the initials AF, had been a part of the furniture of June's life for as long as she could remember. It was dated 1683 and was difficult to read, but I could, with some difficulty, see the words 'Flower, five fire hearths and five shillings'. It was a receipt for the hearth tax. On 25 March 1683 Saltford had five working fireplaces and Collector L2 received the sum of five shillings for the next six months' use of fires. The 25th of March was Lady Day, which had long been a significant date in the life of Saltford. It had begun as the naming day for St Mary's, the holy day of the village, then it became a village holiday and now it was the tax day! The hearth tax was unpopular, not just with those being taxed but also with those doing the taxing, and was soon replaced by a window tax: much easier for collectors to count, with no messy investigations involving complicated tax avoidance, in this case walled-up fireplaces reopened shortly after the visit.

Two of the hearths were downstairs, in the kitchen and the drawing room, and three upstairs in the bedrooms. So the house would have seemed cold by our standards, even when the fires were all lit. A house with enormously thick walls does, however, retain heat very well (as we have discovered), and so relative to other houses the climate in the bedrooms probably seemed quite mild. No better way for the new residents, Lamorock and his wife Susannah, to finish their day than to climb into sheets warmed by a long-handled copper pan, and drift gently off to sleep by the flickering embers of the bedroom fire.

The West Country is often described as sleepy – a yard off the pace set by London – which was one of the things that attracted us to it, but at the close of the seventeenth century it was anything but sleepy. With the Restoration of the monarchy in 1660 there were many who feared a return to the days of Catholicism and the persecution of the past. In 1685 Charles II was succeeded by his younger brother James, known to be a Catholic, and the Duke of Monmouth, Charles's illegitimate son, was persuaded to leave exile in Holland in a bid to overthrow the newly enthroned King. On 11 June, according to a contemporary Royalist account, 'The Duke of Monmouth, Lord Grey and one Ferguson, a phanatick priest, accompanied with about 100 more, arrived in three small vessels hyred or bought in Holland at Lyme in Dorsetshire.'

One of the several thousand West Country men who joined Monmouth, who may himself have been a 'phanatick', was a member of the Flower family, a saddle-maker called William Flower.

Within two weeks of landing at Lyme, Monmouth's army crossed the river at Keynsham, intent on attacking the weakly defended city of Bristol, but now, inexplicably, Monmouth left them dithering around in the meadows. The afternoon brought torrential rain, and as the rebels were drying out their sodden clothes before smoky campfires, a troop of cavalry from the King's army swam across the Avon and scattered them 'away in the night, it being a miserable rainy night, leaving behind them some horses and arms and fifteen pairs of boots in a room they were going to supper in, for we found the cloth and plates and napkins laid very decently'.

Later that same night, demoralised and damp, the rebels splashed their way down Saltford High Street. There were many in the village who had heard their fathers speak of Cromwell and the old days, days of hope and freedom, and doubtless there were some, even on this wretched night, who left the shelter of their homes to catch a glimpse of the swashbuckling Monmouth. It is possible that William and Lamorock spoke during that wet night; perhaps Susannah had prepared some bread and cheese and a flagon of strong ale. But as the rebels left Bath and wheeled back towards mid-Somerset, the direction from which they had just come, it must have been obvious to all but the most partisan that this was an army with no plan, marching with its heart in its boots, which, incidentally, were falling to bits. And so it proved. Within days of their defeat in the peat bogs of Sedgemoor, Monmouth had been executed and the search was on to bring to trial those involved in the rebellion.

The authorities published a list of 4,000 wanted rebels, one of whom was William Flower. William's relation to Lamorock was unclear but men were being hauled into the dock for the flimsiest of reasons and it is certain that no family wanted any relation on the list, far less a family known to support the Protestant cause. There began a series of show trials presided over by a man described as 'behaving more like a Jack-pudding than with the gravity that becomes a Judge . . . very full of jokes upon people who gave evidence'. This is the transcript of a conversation that took place between that 'Jack-pudding' – Judge Jeffreys – and another man who, like William Flower, was suspected of 'aiding'.

LORD CHIEF JUSTICE JEFFREYS: And this is as much as you know of the business?

DUNNE: Yes, my lord, that is all I remember.

JEFFREYS: Well, and what hadst thou for all thy pains?

DUNNE: Nothing but a month's imprisonment, my lord.

JEFFREYS: Thou seemest to be a man of a great deal of kindness and good-nature; for by this story, there was a man that thou never sawest before and because he only had a black beard, and came to thy house, that black beard of his should persuade thee to go twenty-six miles, and give a man half a crown out of thy pocket to show thee the way, and all to carry a message from a man thou never knewest in thy life to a woman thou never sawest in thy life . . . doest thou believe that anyone here believes thee? Prithee what trade art thou?

DUNNE: My lord, I am a baker by trade.

JEFFREYS: And wilt thou bake thy bread at such easy rates? Upon my word then, thou art very kind. Prithee tell me, I believe thou dost use to bake on Sundays, dost thou not?

DUNNE: No, my lord, I do not.

JEFFREYS: Alack-a-day! Thou art very precise in that; but thou canst travel on Sundays to lead rogues into lurking holes. It seemeth thou hast a particular kindness for a black beard, that's all thy reason for undertaking all this trouble. Thou hast told me all the truth, hast thou?

DUNNE: I have, my lord.

JEFFREYS: But I assure thee thy bread is very light weight, it will scarce pass the balance here.

DUNNE: I tell the truth, and nothing but the truth.

JEFFREYS: No doubt of that; but prithee tell me, whose horse didst thou ride when thou wentest first?

DUNNE: The man's horse that came to me to desire me to go to the message.

JEFFREYS: How came he to trust thee with his horse?

DUNNE: The Lord knows, my lord.

JEFFREYS: Thou sayst right, the Lord only knows, for by the little I know of thee I would not trust thee with two-pence. Dost thou take the God of heaven not to be a God of truth, and that He is not a witness of all thou sayst?

DUNNE: My lord, I am so baulked, I do not know what I say myself; tell me what you would have me say for I am clutter'd out of my senses . . .

Dunne was lucky, not so the defendant, a slightly deaf woman in her seventies. She had given lodging to two men who, unknown to her, had been part of the rebel army, and was sentenced to be burnt at the stake, a sentence later changed by the King, who Jeffreys described as 'almost all mercy', to beheading. In the course of the next couple of weeks Jeffreys sent 480 to the gallows, transported 850 to the West Indies and sentenced 260 to be whipped or fined, sometimes dealing with as many as two hundred cases in one day. The hangings were public, as was the burning of entrails, quartering of corpses, boiling in salt and dipping them in pitch for long-term exhibition. The sheriff instructed the mayor of Bath to prepare for executions and printed broadsheets listing names, place of execution and accounts of the costs of placing severed limbs at crossroads, market places and village greens. Saltford almost certainly received some of these parcels of human flesh, posted high above the green next to St Mary's church. Even by the standards of the time this was barbaric and most people were shocked, no matter which side they were on. A landowner protested to the King. He did not have to wait long for an answer – some days later a rebel commander, a man personally known to him, was hanged and chopped up outside his front gate.

Shortly after finishing in Wells, possibly on the evening of his last day's work, village lore has it that Jeffreys spent the night in Saltford in a house less than two minutes' walk from the Manor. It is possible: Saltford is en route from Wells to London, the house in question is dated early to mid-seventeenth century and has for as long as anyone can remember been called Jeffreys Lodge. Perhaps it was an inn or perhaps it was lived in by a member of the local judiciary keen to entertain the great man. It had only been a matter of weeks since the rebel army had limped down this same street and now, under the cover of a different night, Saltford was providing lodging to one of the villains of English history, a man who presided over a sequence of trials so horrifying they are still known today as the Bloody Assizes. As he lay in bed on this, his last night in the West Country, so too, just around the corner, did Lamorock and Susannah. If the current climate continued, and it did – a general pardon was not issued until the following spring – they would need more than the glow of embers in their bedroom fire to keep them safe.

William Flower was never found, certainly not by the authorities. According to a drummer in the Royalist army, writing a journal resting on his drumhead, 1,394 rebel soldiers died besides many lying 'unfound in the corn'. Perhaps his body was amongst those buried in one pit or perhaps he was one of those huddled outside Weston church.

53, tied together.
32, tied together
2, wounded in their legs, crawling upon the ground on their hand and knees,
37 tied and pinnacled together.
1 alone, being naked, only his drawers on.
1 more running, being forced along by two horseman with blows and riding close after him.
46, tied together, such as had a good coat or anything worth the pilling were fairly stripped of it.

A Dutch gunner and a 'Yellow coat soldier' who had deserted the King's army were hanged just before sundown on a tree not far from the church. Five hundred rebel prisoners, many of them fatally wounded, shuffled past their swinging bodies as they were herded into the church, fearful of what the morning would hold. The horrors of that night are best described by this matter-of-fact entry in the parish records:

> For cleansing the church 10 shillings 6 pence
> For frankincense and saltpetre and resin and other things
> to burn in the Church after the prisoners was gone out
> 5 shillings 8 pence

William's fate remains unclear: he fought in the last battle to be fought on English soil and then disappeared without trace; or so it would seem. But no one disappears completely and certainly not in the memories of those who love them. Seven years later, a folk ballad composed in 1692 told the story of a life lived in the shadow of Sedgemoor.

> *Oh Lord, where is my husband now –*
> *Where once he stood beside me?*
> *His body lies at Sedgemoor*
> *In grave of oak and ivy;*
> *Come tell me you who beat the drum,*
> *Why am I so mistreated?*
> *To stand alone, a traitor's wife,*
> *My will to live defeated.*
> *He swore to me he would be gone*
> *For days but two and twenty –*
> *And yet in seven years or more*
> *His bed lies cold and empty.*

It is said that history is written by the winners. That's as may be, Saltford's history had hardly been written by anyone at all: a few lines in Domesday, the odd will and a hearth tax receipt, but now, at this the end of Saltford's most dramatic century, a cry from the heart written by one of history's losers.

# 12

# The Secret Garden

S ALTFORD, exhausted by the events of 1685, nodded off again, leaving four generations of Lamorocks to doze their way through the better part of the eighteenth century. By the time they had woken up, England, or Great Britain as she was now called, had emerged as a superpower, Britannia ruled the waves and, amazingly, the man who was to become June's great-grandfather was crawling around his bedroom some four years *before* Admiral Nelson won the Battle of Trafalgar.

But this is partly a story about land, and great clods of the stuff were now spread like a scab over the trench slashed across the face of our front garden. The place described on the estate agents' details as an 'attractive ornamental garden' was now a van and lorry park for the small army of builders who gathered daily in front of the house. And yet . . . this patch of land, covered with milk cartons and crisp packets, had become for me a sort of wonderland; as if it was a document which had been written on and erased over and over again.

At the beginning of the eighteenth century, a new approach to landscape gardening was emerging. The French style of starburst paths and knot gardens based on the grand formality of the Palace of Versailles, which was previously thought to be the height of fashion, was now seen as restrictive and stuffy. Now it was the landscape just beyond the garden, celebrated for its Englishness, which was to set the tone for what happened inside the garden walls. In 1713, one of the leading style gurus of the time, the poet and enthusiastic garden designer Alexander Pope, published an article in which he poked fun at the pompous formality of the old ideas.

A Citizen is no sooner a Proprietor of a couple of Yews, but
he entertains Thoughts of erecting them into Giants, like
those of a Guild-hall. I know an eminent Cook, who
beautified his Country Seat with a Coronation Dinner in
Greens, where you see the Champion flourishing on
Horseback at one end of the table, and the Queen in
perpetual Youth at the other.

He went on to imagine a fictional catalogue of evergreen plants for sale:

Adam and Eve in yew; Adam a little shattered by the fall
of the tree of Knowledge in the great storm; Eve and the
serpent very flourishing . . .

St George in Box; his arm scarce long enough, but will be
in a condition to stick the dragon by next April.

A green dragon of the same, with a tail of ground-ivy for
the present
NB – these two are not to be sold separately.

An old Maid of honour in wormwood.

Divers eminent modern poets in bays, somewhat
blighted, to be disposed of a penny worth.

Geometrically perfect box and yew hedges were out of tune with
the times. Political stability and economic prosperity encouraged
landowners to look beyond their immediate patch with feelings of
pleasure. Now nature, tamed and enclosed, could be contemplated
with satisfaction. The winds of change were blowing through the
country and nowhere, not even a sleepy village on the banks of the
River Avon, was unaffected. In one of those accidents of geogra-
phy in which Saltford seemed to specialise, the village was caught
up in a conflict, a thing of small importance other than to those
involved, but whose components would be repeated again and
again in the coming years.

Three years before the publication of Pope's article, a scheme
had been launched to make the River Avon navigable by allowing
the passage of barges between Bristol and Bath. In the preamble to
the Act of Parliament it was stated that such a scheme would make

passenger travel 'commodious and convenient for persons of Quality'. Lamorock, great-grandson of Lamorock senior, almost certainly saw himself as a person of quality, but would surely have been opposed to the project. From the earliest times the mill had been a part of the manor estate and eliminating the tidal flow of the waters, the whole point of the scheme, would reduce its power and therefore make it a less desirable asset. In addition to this he owned the lands on either side of the river and like any farmer he would surely have resisted any plan which might lead to the loss of crop-growing land. The local resistance was strong enough to delay the scheme for ten years but the commercial case was overwhelming and inevitably those who opposed it were defeated.

The country's commercial face was changing, the Bank of England had been established just before the new century had begun, and the principle of buying shares in a company – joint-stock companies – was transforming the way people thought about wealth. One such company was formed in December 1724. The first meeting was attended by Bath's leading entrepreneur, a man who had already made his fortune developing a national postal service. This was Ralph Allen, who together with a Bristol timber merchant could see the potential profits in the building boom that was just beginning to hit Bath. The shareholders also included a plumber and glazier, a land developer and a twenty-two-year-old called John Wood, who secured a contract for digging dirt in the 600-yard cut just downstream of Saltford. From this humble beginning (made even more humble by the fact that his contract was terminated), Wood would go on to become the primary architect behind Bath's now-famous crescents and squares.

Lamorock, who had spent the better part of ten years fighting the scheme, was now seventy-five years old – very much yesterday's man. Before the century was over most large towns in England were close to a canal, some owing their very existence to the new waterways. From now on, those living in Saltford who were unable or unwilling to embrace change would increasingly find themselves on the wrong side of a conflict between the past and the future.

The Flowers may have been unhappy but they weren't the only ones. Other more aggressive voices rose against this scheme, those of local miners whose livelihoods were threatened by the cheaper coal coming down the River Severn from Shropshire. Late one night three hundred of them arrived in Saltford armed with metal bars and sledgehammers and set about the lock gates and the newly constructed weir. They damaged them, leaving papers saying that unless an immediate stop was made to sending coal by water a thousand men would return to finish their work. Such incidents became increasingly common as the industrialisation of England gathered pace. A diplomat who had lived in Florence from 1730 to 1780 and was about to return home received a letter from a friend: 'You left England as a private island living upon its means. You will find it the capital of the world.'

Ten days before Christmas of 1727 the first barge, pulled not by horses but by three or four men, passed through Saltford's newly repaired lock carrying timber and pig iron, bound for one of the numerous building projects spread across Bath. Now the supply lines were in place for the city to become the architectural flower of Georgian England.

Cutting into Bath's southern slopes is a steep-sided valley, like a triangle broad at the top and narrowing as it descends towards the city. At its head sits one of the jewels in one of England's most beautiful cities. Prior Park, designed by John Wood, was owned by the same Ralph Allen who had once crossed swords with Lamorock Flower. Since then he had acquired the local Bath stone quarries and in so doing made his second fortune. Allen entertained the great and the good at his new home, among them the composer George Frederick Handel, William Pitt the Elder, the MP for Bath (who went on to become one of the country's great prime ministers), and the writer Henry Fielding, who portrayed him as Squire Allworthy in *Tom Jones*: 'Neither Mr Allworthy's house nor his heart were shut against any part of mankind, but they were particularly open to men of merit. To say the truth, this was the only house in the kingdom where you were sure to gain a dinner by deserving it.'

It may have been easier to get an invitation to dinner at Saltford; certainly the company would have been less intellectual. Lamorock's social circle included his immediate family and friends, who, after the plates had been cleared, might have taken a turn around a garden laid out in plain grass rectangles, divided by sand or gravel paths and bordered with narrow flower beds. In 1739 a publication called *Common Sense* announced that 'Every Man, now, be his fortune what it Will, is to be *doing something* at his Place, as the fashionable Phrase is; and you hardly meet any Body, who, after the first Compliments, does not inform you that he is *in Mortar* and *moving* of Earth.' Lamorock wasn't in mortar, his forefathers had taken good care of all that, but he may well have been in moving of earth; everyone else was. The followers of this new movement saw themselves as painters using plants rather than paint and suggested that there was within every unpromising scene an unseen garden waiting to be unlocked. The most famous landscape gardener of all, Lancelot 'Capability' Brown, gained his nickname because he was said to observe when inspecting a client's property that he could see 'great capability of improvement', a phrase which well described the current condition of the garden at Saltford.

I loved the ivy-covered door in the wall which led to the churchyard. It was something to do with the call of a world beyond. This forgotten little corner was so very 'English', evoking as it did long drinks with slivers of lime and fresh mint, cottage paths and wild flowers. Little wonder that the English abroad often try to recreate the gardens of their homes, since there are few more powerful ways to remind themselves of the old country.

I once heard a story about a man travelling through Sicily who came across a beautifully kept garden, full of flowers that usually only grow in England, like cineraria. Not surprisingly the locals called it 'The English Garden'. Working away in the corner was the gardener. It was early evening, the heat of the day was fading and the two men got talking.

'How long have you worked here?'

'Forty years.'

'Is the owner about?'

'He's away but he'll be back.'

'When?'

'I don't know.'

'How long has it been since you last saw him?'

'I've never seen him.'

'You've worked here for forty years without seeing the owner and you don't know when he's coming back?'

'Yes.'

'But this is one of the most beautiful gardens I've ever seen.'

'Thank you.'

'I would have thought you were expecting him tomorrow.'

'Today, sir. Today.'

Gardens do that to people: they give hope and life. Certainly that was what our garden was giving me. Clumps of daffodils were pushing their yellow way through some of the gaps between the builders' vans. Spring was arriving and not a minute too soon.

And then there were the girls: the main reason for moving out of London in the first place. With each passing day I could see that this garden had been waiting for them, for building dens and going off on adventures to foreign climes with bottles of ginger beer, for making swords out of bits of wood and string. It was, of course, an airbrushed version of my own childhood, drawn from books which were already fifty years old by the time I had been born and which, on reflection, were probably written for June when she was a child. Here the summers would stretch on and on as they did in my own memories. No matter that the pictures evoked had nothing to do with the reality of two girls born in the last decade of the twentieth century; they were helping me get closer to the biggest dream of all – the time when all four of us would actually live here.

If the garden was to be the children's day room, bedroom 3, the room above the kitchen, was going to be their night room. It was on the same floor as our bedroom, just along the landing, not too far away and next to the second bathroom. But it was a sad affair; its glory, the supporting roof timbers, hidden by a low sagging waterlogged ceiling. For the better part of the previous winter, water had been flowing down through the ceiling onto the floorboards below, most of which I had been obliged to rip out. It was now damp and unsafe, a view which Abigail, our four-year-old, clearly shared.

'Where are we going to sleep, Daddy?'

'I'll show you, come with me.' I took her hand and together we mounted the spiral staircase, oak boards on top of the original stone, turned left past the bathroom and stopped in the doorway. The missing floorboards made it dangerous to go any further.

'I thought this room would be nice.' She looked at me in the way children do when they know you are talking complete nonsense. A nastier little room it would have been difficult to imagine.

That night, just before bedtime, the subject came up again.

'Are we all going to sleep in the big house?'

'Yes.'

'When?'

'Soon, really soon, I hope.'

'When we do . . .' She paused before continuing.

'Yes?'

'Could we sleep with you and Mummy?'

'No, no – honestly your room will be lovely, I promise.'

'It's just . . . well, it's not friendly.'

She was right. It was one of the few rooms in the house with no redeeming features. Unless . . . above the sagging ceiling there were water tanks and huge oak A-frames reaching high up to the roof itself . . . unless we pulled down the ceiling and inserted an internal staircase to what would then become a mezzanine floor, the space previously occupied by the water tanks. The idea was not only practical but positively exciting. The room would be crowned by an open framework of oak timbers, some of which were complete with 400-year-old strips of bark. Suddenly it wasn't me trying to find what Alexander Pope called 'the Genius of the place'. It had found me. I envisaged smooth white slopes of plaster spread out between the timbers, a tree house high above the clouds in an alpine forest, and set about drawing up another lighting plot.

And then, within days, in one of those happy accidents of timing which very, very occasionally happen to anyone working with builders, Steve's van pulled up outside the cottage.

'OK if I start on the girls' bedroom on Monday?'

'Fantastic. Thank you so much . . . Any plans for the weekend?'

'I'm off to pick up my lad from his mother's.' His eyes filled with warmth whenever he talked about his son. He was divorced.

'Goin' to take him fishin' – if the weather holds off.'

'Steve, you know those stones you said you wanted for your ponds?'

'Uh-huh.'

'I've been thinking. There's no way I'm ever going to need them all.'

'Are you sure? I thought you said . . .'

'I know. I was wrong.'

He came in for a cup of tea.

After months of visiting the house, watching the sunlight move across the floor, the moment had finally come to share my ideas with the man I had chosen to make them happen. In films I had seen quite ordinary pictures transformed by correctly placed lights, nudging the audience in a particular direction. But this room was no ordinary picture. Now that the timbers were fully exposed, bark and all, anything was possible. Steve listened patiently as he always did, giving nothing away. It was my reference to David Lean and the lighting in *Lawrence of Arabia* that finally drew the proceedings to a halt.

'James – just tell me what you want me to do.'

I did and then, mercifully, we both relaxed. I had taken his dead-pan West Country manner, characterised by zero facial or vocal movement, to mean he did not like me. Perhaps I was wrong. I told him about the girls and my fears about the cost of restoration. He told me how odd it felt to be living with his parents again. It was a funny thing, this relationship, better than the one I had antici-pated. The talk drifted back to his ponds. His son had wanted to know why they had been dug in the corner of a field next to a rail-way line.

'So what did you tell him?'

'I told him there's a lot of stuff we don't know.'

'Was he satisfied with that?'

'No, of course not, he's six.'

Steve was followed by Mark (the plasterer), who in turn was fol-lowed by Brian (the decorator), and the room, for so long the object of my thought-life, was finally finished. Perhaps we really were going to move in before too much longer. Even Simon the Surveyor seemed to think so.

'Just a few more weeks.'

'Simon, come on, that's what you said before Christmas.'

'This time of year everyone wants to crack on – it'll speed up from here on.' We wandered around the garden, pausing to look at the exterior of the house for the hundred and tenth time.

'The great thing is the building's going to be able to breathe – so important to use environmentally friendly materials.'

We wandered over to the hedge overlooking the meadows which ran gently down to the river. I was taken with the idea of 'borrowing' the surrounding landscape, of drawing the meadows into our garden, and suggested ripping out the hedge.

'No,' said Simon, with uncharacteristic resolve.

'Why not? It would look great – and might even impress Bob Sutcliffe.' This was the friendly historical buildings planner who had encouraged us to buy the place on that fateful first visit. 'I've been reading quite a bit of stuff and we might be able to construct a heritage case . . .'

'Yes, I dare say, but Bob and Pat wouldn't like it.'

Bob and Pat were our neighbours and they enjoyed walking their dog up the lane which ran along the hollow between the hedge and the field. Simon was right – and I didn't want to fall out with them before we had even moved in.

'Fair enough – but what about the rest of the back garden?'

'I can put you on to someone who does quite a bit for me – works well with this sort of property.'

I called Simon's man with the intention of checking him out, but in the event he was the one checking me out. It wasn't, he told me, his 'sort of thing'. Where, I wondered, were the Capability Browns of today? Not, I discovered, in the Bath Yellow Pages. Over the next few days I managed to persuade a few people to come and have a look. They scuffed and kicked the ground with varying degrees of confidence, sharing only two things: sky-high quotations and cowboy boots worn outside their trousers. In the end Mike put me in touch with Dennis, a local farmer who arrived in a sensible pair of shoes together with his son Michael, two forks and a bag of grass seed.

The three of us joined Steve and Terry, an old campaigner recruited by Mike, midway through the morning break. Terry had large, capable hanging hands and walked as if on the deck of a rolling ship; like most elderly builders his knees and elbows had been damaged by years 'on the building'. Apart from his ability to put one stone on top of another, which was considerable, he had one quality which I valued highly: he was funny but like Steve he hid his sense of humour under a West Country bluffness that looked, and felt, like hostility.

'What you going to do about the rubbish in the front garden?'

'Clear it and maybe get a landscape architect.'

'Landscape architects!' spat Terry, the cue for everyone to put down their papers. Clearly this was going to be enjoyable. 'Some poncey bloke in a Range Rover turns up with a load of plans . . . ends up with a couple of blokes on the dole digging holes in the ground.'

We never did use a landscape architect; in the end a wheelbarrow and lawnmower seemed to do the trick. To sit in one of Lamorock's window seats and watch the girls run across what is now a proper lawn and hear them shrieking with laughter (surely one of the world's most beautiful sounds) is to feel wonderfully free. Julia, our youngest, recently told me that it was easier to play made-up games in this garden than anywhere else. Perhaps any garden, in any age, is best described in the words of one early gardener as a 'chamber roofed by heaven'.

# 13

# The Gates

J ULY 1750: a flotilla of rowing boats approached the Shallows. The first boat glided towards the river bank, a footman jumped ashore and the passengers stood up and wobbled. This was no easy business, dressed as they were in the uniform of high society; the men were tightly wrapped in brocaded silk, the ladies held fast within corsets.

And so it was that Prince Frederick of Wales, eldest son of George II, came to Saltford for a cup of tea. Tents were rigged and tables set with fine china, the stage set for something called a 'pique nique', a recent import from France adopted by fashionable society, many of whom now came regularly to Bath. And on this long-forgotten afternoon there can have been few more fashionable collections of tea-drinkers than those gathering on the bank of the river at Saltford. Villagers drifted down the hill and the Prince, reading the scene with some skill, ordered that two hogsheads of beer be set out for them. Encouraged by the beer and curious to get a better look at the exotic creatures who had landed in their midst, the villagers pushed forward for a closer view.

Behind the endlessly fluttering fans held by the women (one contemporary said it took three months of practice before the art of fluttering was fully mastered) were faces caked in a foundation of white lead, cheeks rouged with a red leather imported from Brazil, lips coloured with plaster of Paris and eyebrows hidden behind mouse skin. One or two of the company had noticeably rounded cheeks – the product of small cork balls held inside the cheeks which helped the wearers speak with a fashionable lisp. And one was sporting, in the French mode, a false pair of buttocks.

Hair was in the frontline of fashion then just as it is today; indeed the eighties phrase 'big hair' might have been coined for the Georgian age. Hair sat rather like a bouquet on top of the head, decorated with ribbons, blossoms, fruit, feathers and even the flowers of runner beans. There is a contemporary tongue-in-cheek account of 'the acre and a half of shrubbery, kitchen gardens and greenhouses' worn by the fashionable young. For the fashion-conscious man, the choices were equally extravagant. There were story wigs and bob wigs, busby wigs and scratch wigs, bag wigs, brown George wigs, riding wigs, nightcap wigs, periwigs, tie wigs and queue wigs, dark majors, grizzle majors, grizzle ties and several more.

The Prince's party might have had a selection of caraway seed cakes and some sherry-laced plum pudding, both enormously popular. In a strong green China tea caudle there would have been tea leaves, sugar, nutmeg, egg yolk and white wine. But the picnic only really got going when, shortly after the first dishes had been drained, the musicians ripped into a country jig and the two parties merged; dancing, singing and joking. And then, between five and six in the afternoon, the royal party tottered back into the waiting boats, leaving what an eyewitness described as 'a cheering multitude'.

This was *the* moment when Georgian Bath came to Saltford. In a story full of history's extras and walk-ons it was a moment to treasure, the more so because the following spring the Prince died. His life had not amounted to much. His mother and father hated him. His son, the future George III, was unhappier than most on hearing about the death of his father but even he could go no further than to say, 'I feel something here.' Then he put his hand on his heart – a promising gesture, which was rather undone by what he said next: 'Like I did when I saw two workmen fall from the scaffold at Kew.' Even Ralph Allen, who rarely said anything bad about anyone, wrote to a friend that although the Prince seemed to understand quickly things he was told, soon afterwards he 'appeared to know nothing'. Perhaps the most memorable thing about his life was the manner of his death, caused, it was widely believed, by being hit on the head by a cricket ball – a very English death which left the majority of his subjects completely unmoved. He might not have been one of history's shining stars but he did achieve something in death, being the subject of one of the most downbeat epitaphs ever written.

*Here lies poor Fred who was alive and is dead,*
*Had it been his father I had much rather,*
*Had it been his sister nobody would have missed her,*
*Had it been his brother, still better than another,*
*Had it been the whole generation, so much better for the nation,*
*But since it is Fred who was alive and is dead,*
*There is no more to be said.*

But the people of Saltford felt that there *was* something else to be said and they met to discuss how they might remember this man who had been kind to them at the picnic. But there was not much money in Saltford and the villagers, or 'rustics' as my local source insists on calling them, decided that their memorial should take the form of an annual cricket match in the meadow where the picnic had been held. The resolution, explaining the choice of cricket, stated that 'His Royal Highness was a great admirer of the diversion.' And so it was that on Saturday, 13 July 1751, a great cricket match was held 'in memory of his late Highness, Prince Frederick'. This gesture was loyal, kind and flew in the face of public opinion – marvellous qualities, rather too marvellous as it turned out. Within a few years the memorial match had been forgotten.

These were Bath's glory days. But though the world and his wife were beating a path to the city, it was not to everyone's taste. Mrs Montagu, writing to her friend the Duchess of Portland, expressed her dislike of the place:

The morning after I arrived, I went to the Ladies Coffee House, where I heard nothing but the rheumatism in the shoulder, the sciatica in the hip, and the gout in the toe. I began to fancy myself in the hospital of the infirmary . . . I should be glad to send you some news, but all the news of the place would be like bills of mortality, palsy, four, gout, six, fever, one. We hear nothing but Mr Such-a-one is not abroad today; Oh! Says another, poor gentleman, he died to-day. Then another cries, my party was made for quadrille to-night, but one of the gentlemen has had a second stroke of the palsy, and cannot come out; there is no depending upon people, nobody minds engagements. Indeed the only thing one can do to-day, we did not do the day before, is to die.

Still, some people were up and doing. John Wood, the junior engineer who had worked briefly on the Saltford stretch of the Avon navigation scheme, was building some of the loveliest squares and terraces in the country. Even so the best was yet to come. He passed the mantle to his son, John Wood the Younger, who designed what today many consider to be the finest domestic vista in England. In 1775, after eight years of construction, there stood high on the southern slopes of Bath a great curve of thirty identical houses, almost 50 feet high and over 500 feet in length. The buildings are magnificent, fringed by a cobbled street and wide pavement, the whole edifice dropping away in sloping lawns to the hidden river below. The Royal Crescent is the climax of Georgian Bath; there is none finer.

Writing some time later, the novelist Jane Austen, in her novel *Mansfield Park*, touches on builders, landscaping and house improvement.

'I wish you could see Compton,' said Mr Rushworth, 'it is the most complete thing! I never saw a place so altered in my life. I told Smith I did not know where I was. The approach now is one of the finest in the country; you see the house in the most surprising manner. I declare when I got back to Sotherton yesterday, it looked like a prison – quite a dismal old prison.'

'Oh, for shame!' cried Mrs Norris. 'A prison, indeed! Sotherton Court is the noblest old place in the world.'

'It wants improvement, ma'am, beyond anything. I never saw a place that wanted so much improvement in my life; and it is so forlorn, that I do not know what can be done with it.'

'Your best friend upon such an occasion,' said Miss Bertram calmly, 'would be Mr Repton, I imagine.'

'That is what I was thinking of. As he has done so well by Smith, I think I had better have him at once. His terms are five guineas a day.'

'Well, and if they were ten,' cried Mrs Norris, 'I am sure you need not regard it. The expense need not be any impediment. If I were you, I should not think of the expense, I would have everything done in the best style, and made as nice as possible. Such a place as Sotherton Court deserves everything that taste and money can do. You have space to work upon there, and grounds that will reward you. For my part, if I had anything within the fiftieth part of the size of Sotherton, I should always be planting and improving, for naturally I am excessively fond of it . . .'

Now, almost for the first time, I had a picture with a soundtrack, albeit one that could not be taken too literally. Nevertheless, given that Saltford had not had any major work for well over a hundred years, it is perfectly possible that it did look like 'a dismal old prison'. Certainly that was how it looked when Anna and I had first seen it. But what we do know, because the evidence remains to be seen, is that at some point during the latter part of the eighteenth century the approach to Saltford was altered to include a classic pair of Georgian gates.

Ironically, in the light of all the novels written during this time, this was the moment when my previous source, the Register of Wills, went temporarily silent. During the Second World War the records for this period had been moved from Taunton to Exeter because it was thought that Exeter was a safer place. Bad move – Hitler's bombs destroyed them. But fortunately amongst my growing archives I found a sheet of paper, yellow and faded, which set out the bare bones, just dates and names of Saltford's owners during the eighteenth and nineteenth centuries. George Flower was born in 1753 and died in 1809. He was to see the decline of the old agricultural England, as well as the beginnings of the Empire and modern industrial England, and so he was therefore a significant figure in the story of the house.

Could he have been anything like one of Henry Fielding's characters, whose custom it was every afternoon 'as soon as he was drunk, to hear his daughter play on the harpsichord'? Such men threw themselves into singing 'Rule, Britannia!' and rejoiced in the victories of the British army who were conquering the known and unknown world, haphazardly painting the map red. They were violently opposed to the government's proposal for a national census on the grounds that it would provide dangerous information for enemies abroad and at home, whom they called 'placemen and taxmasters'. Rather than provide an account of their homes and their families, they instructed their servants to show interfering government officials 'the discipline of the horse-pond'.

An uncomfortable possibility was emerging. The new owner of Saltford might have had something in common with John Bull, a popular cartoon character who emerged a few years later. John Bull, whose shape I recalled from childhood printing sets, was as wide as he was high and dressed in a Union Jack waistcoat. He had no time for foreigners, especially the French, and was never happier than when sitting in front of a full plate of English beef and a bottle of beer. I wondered if the picture I had been building up – a succession of owners noted for their sincerity and family values – was just a little too good to be true.

But whatever the truth about the new owner's character, it occurred to me that in the matter of the gates we had something in common. After all, only a few months earlier I had said that I had no aspirations to live in a house with the trappings of 'Manordom', but just recently, unknown to Anna, I had found myself revisiting our plans for the gates at the bottom of the drive, the ones she had found so absurdly grand on our first visit. From the first moment she had felt that there was no way she could live behind them. And so we had decided that we would change the entrance into something more modest. But all that was months ago. Now, contrary to everything we had agreed, I had begun to feel that rather than taking down the gold letters announcing SALTFORD MANOR to the world on the grounds that they were too showy, we should give them a fresh coat of paint. Surely a house like Saltford *deserved* a proper set of Georgian gates? Coming from a London house where our unimposing front door opened onto the pavement, I had begun to think that perhaps a little grandeur wouldn't go amiss.

The black laced wrought-iron gates stood high and proud; and on top of the pillars were a huge pair of Victorian gas lamps now converted for electricity. But while my feelings about the gates had softened, Anna's appeared to have hardened, and indeed spread to include the lamps which she also wanted removed. And so it was that I met with Simon the Surveyor to discuss the practicalities. Anna clearly felt she had conveyed her views to me forcibly enough to let me undertake the discussion without her. We walked down the drive and stood with our backs to the High Street.

'We want to make the entrance less formal.'

'What is it exactly you don't like?'

'It's all too much of a "statement" – I can almost hear the fanfare.'

Simon dropped his eyes and nodded, trying to agree when he clearly didn't. He was a master of this look, wheeling it out whenever there was a difference of opinion.

'OK – so what would you like to see?'

'Well, I thought one of those five-bar wooden gates, the sort you see in a field.'

'But this is the Manor – I'm just not sure what the village would say.'

'Does it matter? It is our house.'

'Yes, of course, but it's not just them, there's English Heritage to think about.'

'Simon, let's not beat around the bush – can they stop us? The gates aren't listed are they?'

'No, probably not, but they would be seen as coming within the curtilage of the main property.'

'The what?'

'The enclosed land next to the house itself . . . any changes we make within the parcel must be fitting with the style of property.'

'Are you saying that some guy in London is able to tell me what sort of gates I am able to have?'

'Yes.'

'That's mad – why?'

'Because in heritage terms you are just passing through – they see you as the custodian. This is an important house – whatever changes we make have to be consistent with the history of the place.'

'Are we supposed to keep the place as some sort of museum?'

It seemed wrong that a man in London who was completely indifferent to Saltford, and who offered us no money to help improve the place, had the power to stop us having the kind of gates we (or at least Anna) wanted. Perhaps it was at just such a moment that men like George threatened to show the men from London 'the discipline of the horse-pond'. But times have changed – although not, it seemed, the feelings of home-owners – and I understood that arguing with Simon was a waste of time. He was not going to fall out with English Heritage, whose opinions would be important to him long after we had moved in.

'How would it be if we kept the gates but removed the letters and the lamps, would that be OK?'

'Probably, but I suggest that you keep both so that if you have second thoughts you could reinstate them.'

'No, we wouldn't want to do that.'

'I know, but best to be safe.'

And so it was that I turned to the handbook of historical house restoration, the Bath Yellow Pages, and phoned a company called Iron Art listed as specialising in bespoke restoration work.

John arrived in a van and a flurry of self-promotion. We chatted about his house, his sculptures, his dog grates and his personalised garden furniture; eventually, by the time we had finally reached the end of his presentation, we had arrived at the bottom of the drive.

'I want to rip out the gold letters and chop off the lamps.'

'Why's that then?'

'I think they're too much.'

'Fair enough – they're your gates . . . It's just that most of our work goes the other way.'

'How do you mean?'

'Well, most people want to make the new look old. You're going the other way and if you ask me . . .'

'Don't tell me, you think they're great?'

'Well, yes I do – you'd have to go a long way to find work as fine as this. The lamps are quite exceptional – late Victorian, wonderful.'

'You think so?'

'I know so – but hey, I'm here to do a job – you say the word and I'll get cracking.'

And so he did. After half an hour of hacking and tugging we carried both lamps and a barrowful of gold letters up to the garage for storage.

The picture on the box for the new lamps had looked fine. Plain glass panels, framed by thin metal frames on a simple stand. Not hugely different from the lamps we had just removed, only much smaller. On a shelf in Homebase, surrounded by other similar lamps, they had looked suitably modest, even stylish. Back in Saltford, offered up next to massive gates, sitting on the wide stretch of wall that separated Queen Square from the front garden, they looked comic. Never in the field of exterior lighting had two lamps looked so wrong. Anna and I both agreed that in the circumstances the only thing to be done was to put the old lamps back.

I called John, taking some comfort that his ad had said he did restoration work, and was relieved to get his answerphone.

'Thank you for calling Iron Art. We are not able to get to the phone right now but do leave a message.'

'Hi John – it's James, the man with the lamps. Just calling to say thanks – you did a great job and also . . . um [long pause] . . . I was wondering if you were free next week? It's . . . um – it's a bit difficult to explain.'

# · 14 ·

# A Tale of Two Sketches

J ULY 1789: the Union Jack was flying over Saltford and over
vast chunks of the known world; Clive had conquered India,
Captain Cook had landed in Australia and an unknown artist
had set up his easel in St Mary's churchyard and created a sketch
in Indian ink. The events in France during July could hardly have
been more epic. The 14th of July 1789, the day the Paris mob
stormed the Bastille, marked the start of a revolution in France –
whose battle cry was 'liberty, equality and fraternity'. Not that, on
the meagre evidence of this sketch, much of those were to be had in
Saltford, unless you count the fraternity of the graveyard.

As a piece of art it was unexceptional, or it would not have lan-
guished in the bowels of the British Museum for over two hundred
years. It was weak on action, the only movement the gentle flutter
of a flag held between the paws of a weathered stone lion; and it
was weaker still on human interest, the only people in this particular scene being dead. And yet in spite of its shortcomings, it
became to me a thing of wonder – like looking at a photograph
taken over two hundred years ago. It would be wonderful to be able
to look through the windows and see the family preparing for bed:
the children's feet were being washed and beds beaten and stirred.
Beds were difficult to keep clean; mattresses were organic and were
consequently a paradise for bugs. The *Young Woman's Companion* suggested that its readers, women like twenty-one-year-old Ann Flower,
Saltford's new mistress, 'Set open the windows of the bedchambers
and uncover the beds to sweeten them; which will be a great help
against bugs and fleas . . . Spunge with a mixture of wine, spirit of
turpentine and camphire.' And then when the windows had been
shut and the curtains drawn, to keep out evening draughts and offer

protection from the harmful effects of moonlight, she left a 'night-light' and withdrew downstairs. Perhaps she returned later in the evening for the pleasure of looking at the children asleep.

George was in the larder struggling with a jar of potted venison. Peeling off the leather top, he scraped off the sealing layer of clari-fied fat and cut the contents into thick slices. It was nine o'clock, he had already had the day's main meal – roasted pig and turnips swimming in enough butter to have drowned the pig had it been alive. The inhabitants of substantial houses like Saltford had sub-stantial meals and for the most part became, well . . . substantial. No pen-and-ink sketches of them, no clothes measurements – just a hunch. New techniques of winter feeding for animals meant that it was no longer necessary to kill them in the autumn; so high-quality fresh meat was now available throughout the year. George spooned some pickled spring onions from another jar, placed a loaf of the finest white bread together with a bottle of Spanish wine on a silver platter and took up his customary place in front of Walter's fire.

There was, according to one foreign visitor to England, 'a way of roasting slices of buttered bread before the fire which is incompara-ble. One slice after another is taken and held to the fire with a fork till the butter soaks through the whole pile of slices. This is called toast.' Toast was, in fact, an English invention. Whether George really was a glutton for buttered toast, we will never know. What we do know is that those, like him, who did not have to worry about where their next meal was coming from ate too much meat, too few vegetables and far too many puddings. Currant pond pud-dings, currant suet puddings, butter pudding cake, apple dumplings, plum puddings, plain puddings, plain batter puddings . . . most tables were creaking under the weight of butter and pud-dings, or so it seemed to another foreigner: 'They bake them in the oven, they boil them with the meat, they make them 50 several ways: BLESSED BE HE THAT HATH INVENTED PUDDING, for it is a manna that hits the palates of all sorts of people . . . [and they] are never weary of it.' Such massive amounts of protein and animal fat without fibrous vegetables or coarse bread meant that degenerative diseases such as gout, diabetes, bleeding piles and apoplexy were common. If George had gout, and most men of his class did, he would have taken some water gruel (oats soaked in water and yes, you guessed it – more butter!) just before bed.

George's bedtime practice probably followed a habitual pattern. He would wake the dogs and turn them out into the night, bolt and bar the doors, backside and foreside, as if in preparation for an impending break-in. Although it was safer than in times gone by, in a house like Saltford, *the* house of the village, the threat of thieves was never far away. And then, when all was safely battened down, he padded up the stairs just as he had done every night of his life, oak boards moulded by generations of feet. Four paces, two more steps and he was in the bedroom – rinsing his hands in the white porcelain basin with water drawn from the well in the garden, wiping a linen cloth across his face, attempting as best he could to remove the dust of the day, a difficult job given that the cloth was bone-dry. Water, it was thought, made the skin too sensitive. He undressed quickly, slipped into a long nightshirt, checked that his chamberpot had been correctly positioned by reaching under the bed with his foot, and satisfied that all was well, hauled himself up onto the new horsehair mattress (the children had cow's-hair) which lay spread across the four-poster bed. George and Ann's bed would have faced the fireplace, which he had banked up for the night. The great thing was to keep out the dreaded properties of night-time draughts. People were known to tie their hands under the bedclothes so as to force them to remain in the warm and not stray above the bedding where they could get cold and wake them.

The next morning the two housemaids collected the chamberpots (one for each member of the family) and took them to the 'Jericho', one of the outbuildings in the back garden, also known, rather less biblically, as the necessary house. The architecture was simple enough, four walls and a cesspit just below the seat. The toilet arrangements had not changed in hundreds of years, but a new gentility was creeping into domestic life in preparation for an era in which the home would become ever more important. There would be no more pissing in chimneys or finding the lady of the house, as Samuel Pepys had done a hundred years earlier, alone in the dining room 'doing something on a pot'. George's pot, like Ann's, was a handsome porcelain affair contained within a night-commode, essentially a box on legs, which served to disguise its function and contents and had the added advantage of preventing it freezing up under the bed in winter.

The eighteenth century was the age of the club and the coffee house, and nowhere more so than in Bath, the playground par excellence of the fashionable rich. But a new age was coming, a more private age, when the home would be seen as a shelter, the centre from which men could go out and do manly things. And the particular manly thing that George had gone out and done was to pay £933 for an additional 100 acres of land, an acquisition which reflected what was happening across the country. Farmers were parcelling land into larger and larger units in order to take advantage of the economies of scale made possible by new techniques which had been developed by men like Jethro Tull and Turnip Townsend. The enclosure of land, of which George's acquisition was one tiny part, ruined those families who relied on the common land for grazing their animals, collecting fuel and thatching their homes. Men and women who only a generation ago expected to see out their days in Saltford were forced to leave in order to seek work elsewhere. For many the choice was stark: stay and starve or go.

And so they went – many of them to nearby Bristol, a filthy, smoky sprawl of factories, furnaces, chimneys and sweatshops. On arrival many families were forced to share a room in a lodging house. One of these, a room 18 feet by 10 feet, was recorded as housing twenty-seven adults of both sexes, thirty-one children and numerous dogs. In wet weather, and there was plenty of it, children, always the most vulnerable, slept amongst this mass of damp humanity in soaking clothes. Many died of rheumatic fever or pneumonia. Those not able to get into a lodging house wandered about the streets at night, lying under railway aches, in cellars or under tarpaulins in the docks. Hardly surprising, therefore, that Bristol was recorded as having one of the highest mortality rates in the country.

There were few families who could survive without the wages of all their able-bodied members, so children often began working at five years old. One or two of the Saltford boys might well have secured placements as a chimney sweep's climbing boys. In 1778 a law had been passed which said that the fees payable for a chimney-sweeping apprenticeship should be paid in two instalments, thus ensuring the sweep had an interest in keeping the boy alive until the second instalment was paid. Although they were half-starved to keep them thin enough to climb up narrow chimneys, they often got stuck. Some were suffocated, others burnt; many died. Those children unable to find work stalked the customers who tottered out of the public houses, robbing those who fell unconscious in the street, stole lead and gas pipes from housing sites and swarmed over the sprawling dockside, grabbing whatever they could lay their hands on.

There were sugar factories, glass factories, and brass works – all belching out toxic fumes and smoke. In Birmingham the poet Robert Southey, one of those much taken by the events of 1789, found that every man had a complexion 'composed of oil and dust smoke-dried'. He went on to describe those leaving a local brass works as having red eyes and green hair, the eyes made red by the insufferable heat and the hair turned green by the chemicals. Factory foremen ensured that men did not arrive late for work nor leave early, which in the case of many meant after five o'clock in the morning or before eight o'clock at night. Tired workers lost arms and legs, fingers and toes to primitive unguarded machinery.

The story of these years is in part a story of dispute between employer and employee, a dispute which was as brutal in the country as it was in the city. A farmer's son had noticed that in the wool districts of Somerset the relationship of employer and employee was often 'much nearer to that of a Planter and Slave . . . than might be expected in such a Country as England'. Farmers were laying off men, confident that the overseer of the parish poor would be able to provide workers at lower rates of pay. Throughout the country farmers were making huge amounts of money out of their communities and £933 suggests that George Flower, stomach stretching the contours of his greatcoat, may well have been amongst them.

But there was another farmer, the son of the man who had picnicked in Saltford some forty years earlier.

There is a sketch which shows George III, otherwise known as 'Farmer George', and his wife returning to Windsor from market. The outline of Windsor Castle, flying what is presumably the Union Jack, can just be seen on the left. The King loved the countryside and had created three farms in Windsor Great Park. He took an active interest in their management, and wrote letters under the name of Ralph Robinson, one of his shepherds, to the *Annals of Agriculture*, a sort of Georgian *Farmers Weekly*. He would regularly set off around his estate, stroll into his workers' cottages, alarming them by the abruptness of his manner but winning them over with his kindness. On one such walkabout he came across a small boy.

'Who are you?'

'I be pig boy but I don't work. They want lads here. All this belongs hereabouts to Georgy.'

'Pray, who is Georgy?'

'He is King and lives in castle, but he does no good to me.'

The King, so the story goes, saw to it the boy was given work on one of his farms. Another time he asked a woman working alone in one of his fields, 'Where has everyone gone?' They had all gone to see the King, she said. 'I wouldn't give a pin to see him. Besides, the fools will lose a day's work by it, and that is more than I can afford to do. I have five children to work for.'

'Well then,' said George, putting some money into her hand, 'you may tell your companions who are gone to see the King that the King came to see you.' The gesture would have been kind at any time but was especially kind now, when a combination of poor harvests coupled with massive rises in the price of wheat (47 shillings per quarter in 1789, 160 shillings in 1801) meant that many were facing starvation. George, typically, gave orders that the bread used in the royal household should be made of mixed wheat and rye. It is unlikely, on the evidence of his recent acquisition, that George Flower showed anything like the same concern for his fellow creatures.

But elsewhere the story was very different. There emerged a movement of passionate Englishmen who spoke about inequality and the abuse of child workers, of 'dark satanic mills' and the need for a new beginning. On the day that the artist was sketching Saltford, a nineteen-year-old boy, marked out for a life as a clergyman, was studying at Cambridge University. Some years later, the boy, who left without distinction, would become one of the greatest English poets of all time. Recalling his feelings of the time, he wrote:

> *Bliss was it in that dawn to be alive*
> *But to be young was very heaven!*

Wordsworth got it right – new beginnings have the potential to be heavenly. We had left London hoping that this house might offer us all – young and not so young – a new dawn. Our longing for a new start had wrapped itself around Abigail and Julia and much, perhaps most, of our conversation in those early months revolved around how we could provide a home which they might grow to love. There was, I now think, a sort of madness in all of this. Why were we sending for catalogues of environmentally friendly garden swings when we hadn't yet got a cooker or a bath? No wonder this whole moving-to-the-country business was such a strain.

# 15

# Twenty-One Trees and a Pair of Muddy Boots

F OR THE FIRST fifteen years of the nineteenth century the history of Europe was the history of one man: Napoleon Bonaparte. Once again, England was at war with France and the words of 'Rule, Britannia!', 'Britons never, never, *never* shall be slaves', echoed around the dining rooms of England, rooms owned by the kind of roast-beef-and-plum-pudding men I imagined George Flower to have been. It's possible that George, ever the patriot, exchanged his old chamber pot for one of the newly fashionable ones with flowers on the outside and a picture of the dreaded Napoleon on the inside. But in any event in 1801 George, at the ripe old age of fifty-two, had a son who he called Lamorock – just to be sure. Lamorock never married but lived in the house with his brother Thomas for the better part of the next eighty years and it fell to him to steer the house through what was, arguably, its lowest time.

The impact of the war was considerable, food prices rose sharply and farming communities (sixty out of the sixty-six families living in Saltford were smallholders or farm workers) were heavily hit. To make matters worse, many of these families worked tiny parcels of land which were protected by ancient agreements, some of which went back hundreds of years. Saltford had become a victim of its own heritage. There were to be no new agricultural technologies here – the fields were not big enough. In the post-harvest haze of a July evening the patchwork of stubble and golden hayricks looked much as it does today. But all was not well, not in Saltford, and not, according to one commentator, in the country at large.

William Cobbett maintained that contrary to the stories of national abundance – Britannia the Bountiful bestowing her blessings on those lucky enough to be born within the compass of her skirts – England was actually a land of poverty. In Somerset he found the poor had been forced to sell their best clothes, their blankets and sheets, their looms and any little piece of furniture. He was a man on a mission, intent on uncovering the conditions in which ordinary people were living, and took off around the country, poking into the barnyards and poorhouses, reporting his findings in his paper. It was firecracker journalism, the language of the uneducated man printed, so it seemed, to be read aloud in an inn, on the roof of a mail coach, in the queue which formed at the village pump first thing in the morning. 'I asked how he got on. He said very badly. I asked him, "What was the cause of it?" He said, "Hard times." "What times?" said I, "Was there ever a finer summer, a finer harvest . . .?" "Ah," said he, "they make it bad for people for all that."' Cobbett's publication sold, at the height of its popularity, 66,000 copies per week, massively more than any other publication.

The farmers had, according to Cobbett, been infected by the new money-making creed which was sweeping across the country polluting every*thing* and every*one* it touched. Farmhouses now had within them a

> mistress who is stuck up in a place she calls a parlour, with, if she have children, the 'young ladies and gentlemen' about her: some showy chairs and a sofa (a sofa by all means): half a dozen prints in gilt frames hanging up: some swinging book shelves with novels and tracts upon them: a dinner brought in by a girl that is perhaps better 'educated' than she: two or three nick-nacks to eat instead of a piece of bacon and a pudding: the house too neat for a dirty-shoed carter to be allowed to come into; and everything proclaiming to a sensible beholder, that there is here a constant anxiety to make a show not warranted by the reality. The children (which is the worst of it) are all too clever to work: they are all gentlefolks.

The rural poverty which he saw all around him was, he argued, a direct consequence of these new gentrified aspirations. 'Since the pianofortes and parlour bells and the carpets came into the farmhouse, the lot of the labourers has been growing worse and worse.' He could have been writing about Saltford. Certainly there were carpets and parlour bells in the house, there may even have been a piano. And then in 1821, with the war with France long since won, another event took place in the churchyard; a small thing but one which suggested that even the Flowers might have been putting on some airs and graces.

> Planted in Saltford churchyard January 25th 1821 – 21 trees including 'yew'.
> Present: Master C E L Wightman, Mrs. Flower, Mr. Flower, Misses Ann and Phyliss Flower and Miss Clarke from Bath.

Apart from these few words, there was nothing much to go on, just shadows and shapes, half-remembered images from films and programmes set in the early years of the nineteenth century. Jane Austen, an author whose work has provided more than her fair share of such images, whose stories are forever being filmed, often in Bath itself, gave one of her heroines the famous line, 'It was a sweet view – sweet to the eye and the mind. English verdure, English culture, English comfort . . .' Her words, written with another scene in mind, could perhaps be borrowed to describe this tree-planting scene taking place in St Mary's churchyard. Mr and Mrs Flower, who like Mr and Mrs Bennett in *Pride and Prejudice* (the third edition of which had been published four years earlier) were struggling to make ends meet. Gathered around them were their two daughters and a friend from Bath. Perhaps the friend, Miss Clarke, offered the Flower girls an entrée into Bath's famously fashionable society.

The cloaks which the ladies wore to keep warm disguised the fact that their waists, which had been rising for a number of years, had now reached the point immediately below their bosoms, beyond which they could rise no further. A wide sash, tied in a bow at the back, defined the waistline, the look now that of a long thin pencil; plain lightweight peach or creamy dresses, some embroidery on the hem, bodice and sleeve, a style which surely flattered very few women. Their hair, released from the powder and tortures of earlier times, now fell naturally from under a bonnet which was tied under the chin with a fluttery ribbon.

Today these clothes seem stiff but to Ann and Phyliss Flower they represented a new informality in tune with the new romantic ideas about freedom. Not of course that the two girls standing in St Mary's churchyard were representing anything, but fashion reflects the spirit of the time, and here in Saltford the colour of this spirit, if spirits can be said to have colours, was undeniably green. The Flowers had chosen to spend what must have been some considerable time in the depth of winter *planting trees* for heaven's sake! Nature, fresh air, trees, lightweight dresses made of sprigged cotton and muslin; all, perhaps, pointing to some new thing.

So far so new, so elegant and so, well, it has to be said . . . so BBC. But, and this is one of the scenes the director would have wanted to cover well, the Flowers had been joined by the son of Saltford's parson, none other than Master C.E.L. Wightman. It is tempting to think that Master Wightman might have had designs on one of the Flower girls, a prospect which could well have sent Mrs Flower into a flutter. He was very much the country gentleman in his father's greatcoat which with its multiple shoulder capes looked, he thought, becomingly important. Perhaps it stopped just short of his clean leather boots, which were actually several sizes too big but had fashionably curved tops and tassels. Possibly he was hoping for an invitation to the Manor after the tiresome business with the trees had been completed. Of course the reality may have been rather different: Master Wightman, wearing clodhopping boots and armed with a spade, was part of this little gathering because his father had caught a chill and was not able to venture out and plant the trees himself.

But, significantly, these trees were being planted on the edge of Bath in the heart of Jane Austen country; she was Bath's most famous resident and those who ventured into the city, as the Flower girls surely did, would have been struck by its beauty. The builders had gone, the stone once pale and creamy had turned mellow and golden, and the sharpness had softened. Gone too were the royalty and duchesses of former times, and what remained were just the shades of former glory, but even the shades of glory look good if you are an eighteen-year-old girl living in a village where the most eligible male is the son of the local parson.

The Flower girls probably thought themselves fortunate to live in such informal times and yet the codes of conduct for romance in their society were, to our eyes, heavily restrictive. If Ann and Phyliss were asked to dance they would have been unable to address the man by his Christian name, unable to be alone with him for any period of time and unable to write to him or exchange gifts. According to this code, the relationship, if that is what it became, was to be conducted without any kind of intimacy.

But romance can blossom in the most constrained of circumstances. Twice a week the Assembly Rooms were surrounded by horse-drawn carriages and filled with people flowing along lime-flagged passages, catching glimpses of themselves in handsome candlelit mirrors. Eyes glistened and hearts skipped beats, especially in the ball room. Ann and Phyliss would have stepped out onto the specially chalked floor and joined the two long lines forming down the centre of the room as the musicians struck up. A few steps, a few words, spoken perhaps over a shoulder or under an uplifted arm, all lit by five crystal chandeliers containing literally hundreds of candles.

It was, if the films are to be believed, an elegant world. But are the films to be believed? Not, it seems, on the evidence of what was happening back in Saltford. In films we forget bad smells, toothache, poverty and fear of death in childbirth, the producers understanding that most audiences want to be taken, at least for a short time, to a more attractive place than the one they currently inhabit. Perhaps William Cobbett was right to say that carpets and pianos (and by implication tree planting) showed the countryside was changing for the worse but wrong to automatically assume it was now peopled with 'great parcels of swaggering fellows going about, with vulgarity printed on their countenances, but with good clothes on their backs'. Compared to the majority of the villagers, the Flowers were extremely comfortable, but it is not fair to think of them as swaggering about the village concerned only with their own welfare.

In 1827 the Earl of Shaftesbury (who went on to campaign for children working in factories) had recently been elected as a Member of Parliament, and Lamorock Flower, for his part, had recently been elected as a churchwarden. This was hardly headline news, except, as it turned out, for those in the village who were destitute. The movement to reform, to create a fairer England, was helped on its way by a new surge of what the historians call 'religious enthusiasm', a strangely unattractive term, but one which was breaking out amongst the middle classes.

Becoming a Church of England minister, or obtaining a living as it was quaintly called, was not a matter of being ordained and applying to a central selection body as it is today. The cathedral, the universities and the Crown all had livings to dispose of but by far the greatest number were in the gift of private landowners who bought and sold these livings as investment vehicles. Pluralism – having the care of more than one parish – was common at the time. So was absenteeism – in 1809 there were 11,194 ordained ministers in England, 7,358 of whom were not resident in their parish. And yet for all the glaring weaknesses of the system, for the most part, in most villages, and for most people, it worked quite well.

In times gone by the Manor and the church had been *the* places of the village and a part of both buildings, perhaps the most important part, was in a sense owned by the village. The Lord of the Manor, a title which rather flattered Lamorock's circumstances, was expected to see that his farmhands did not starve. He was expected to give clothes, food and perhaps money to the parish poor, at Christmas and in times of bad harvests or unemployment. In the same way the rector, like a monk of old, was also expected to look after the poor. Many of them had an open-door policy and kept a medicine box in their homes from which to dispense remedies. They took collections of money at the church door after Communion services and then when the congregation had left, stepped outside and distributed the money to the ragged groups huddled against the walls.

It is impossible to know how seriously Lamorock took his responsibilities and whether he liked John Wightman or merely tolerated him. But what we do know, because the parish records tell us so, is that on Saturday, 10 October 1827, he was in a vestry meeting in St Mary's church – the vestry being the bit of the church where the vicar now hangs his robes – meeting the Reverend John Wightman and the overseers of the poor, one of whom had, until recently, been his cousin George. The meeting was probably nothing very special, with those present keen to get away to something more interesting, and certainly the record of what took place sounds commonplace. It was decided to raise a quarterly rate of three pence from each household and to use the money to help those in need. The parish register, previously silent, takes up the story.

> Freeman washing, mending and clothes, as Mrs. Mills find him, and food and lodging for his son. Smock frock and pair of shoes for Mr. Freeman. 14 shillings

> Freeman's clothes, 4 shirts, 4 pairs of stockings. 4 smock frocks, 2 hats, 2 pair of breeches £2 5 shillings and 6 pence.

> Paul Evans for the funeral of child 10 shillings
> Paid Susan Evans for James Hill's child £1
> Expenses for taking the late Thomas Evans out of the River Avon – 'caring' – carrying to church, witnesses and sending to coroners £1 10

> For payment made by George Flower, late overseer, towards the maintenance of a female 'bastard' child – called S Pike – at 1 shilling 6 pence per week – £3.
> Sarah Pike 13 weeks at 3 shillings 6 pence

> Complete change of wearing apparel, a new bedstead and bedding for Betty Brookman
> Washing Brookman's sheets 6 pence
> Bed tucking for Brookman and putting on 2 shillings
> Sarah Hendy – cleaning Poor House and cleaning David Brookman and wife, with different expenses £1.0.0.

Brookman, Pike, Evans, Freeman – names in an obscure register, not to be found on the gravestones in St Mary's churchyard – were best described, to use the language of the time, as paupers.

Social reforms were inevitable; commissioners were sent out from London to investigate the conditions in the village poor-houses and found, somewhat improbably, that 'the whole body of inmates subsisted on food far exceeding . . . not merely the diet of the independent labourer, but that of the majority of the persons who contribute to their support'. It was difficult to believe that Thomas Evans, who had drowned himself in the Avon, had really been eating better food than Lamorock Flower; more likely that the commissioners had been told what to find before they left London. In any event Parliament passed a Poor Law Amendment Act and building began on a new workhouse which was to serve the villages for miles around; no bed tucking for Betty Brookman at the Union.

The Union Workhouse, now Keynsham Hospital, was an unhappy affair. It sat behind a high wall, built for the poor and for the dead – part workhouse, part morgue. In the event the inhabitants of the new workhouses were not the able-bodied poor thought to be 'exploiting' the old system but rather the old, sick, orphaned children, the handicapped, and unmarried or abandoned mothers.

On arrival inmates were stripped, scrubbed down and given standard-issue clothing: corduroy trousers and heavy boots for the men, long skirts and striped aprons for the women. Underclothing was not provided. The diet of all children under nine was to be decided 'at discretion' – Oliver Twist was surely not the only small boy to ask for more. But perhaps worst of all, children were separated from their parents, husbands from their wives, each sleeping in different house blocks – something the inmates resented and which we, with our child-orientated views, find almost impossible to comprehend.

The Union in Bath described itself as 'a well-regulated workhouse, in which he [the pauper] is kept clean and well-clothed; is under a warm roof, and with abundance of companions; out of harm's way and far from the most prolific source of pauperism, the beer-house or gin-shop; and also in the way of receiving good from the regular ministrations of the Chaplain, and from the sobriety and regularity which he is obliged to lead, until a time he acquires a habit of order and decorum'. Another contemporary source makes the same point but in dialogue:

STRAIGHT MAN: 'What did you think of the workhouse when you first entered it?'

VISITING DIGNITARY: 'I was astonished at the excellent food and good things for the inmates. I would not desire better provisions for my own family.'

If these accounts were to be believed then the new workhouses were recreational havens – notwithstanding the fact that the one in Bath slept 88 boys four to a bed, had one bedroom, one school-room and one lavatory!

Meantime the countryside was changing, although in Saltford the changes were so subtle that most of them took place under-ground. The summer of 1836 saw some of the village's oldest and weakest members leave and another much larger, tougher group arrive at the crack of dawn on rattling wagons full of shovels and pickaxes. These men, and others like them, were about to change the face of England and yet the parish records, recently so ful-some about Betty Brookman's sheets, were frustratingly silent about them. How many came to Saltford? How long did they stay and where exactly did they site their huts, some of which slept as many as thirty men, women and children, one above the other in tiers of bunks?

They had come to dig a tunnel under the High Street, a tunnel which was to carry one of the earliest sections of the Great Western Railway between Bristol and Bath. I wandered out across the fields to look at what I had considered to be an ordinary embankment and tunnel – ordinary, that is, until now when I saw them through the eyes of a man armed only with a pick, shovel and wheelbarrow. The men who built the tunnel must have been astonishing. They were required to shift 20 tons of earth and rock each day, often bal-ancing wheelbarrows on wet planks laid up impossibly steep slopes. Certainly they drank plenty, ten pints of strong ale a day was nor-mal; they ate plenty, consuming at least two pounds of meat and two pounds of bread each day; and they were followed about by young women who slept with them and older women who did their cooking – many women, few wives.

And yet navvies (the name given to these railway labourers) were, according to one of their number, misunderstood. They were 'wonderfully tender-hearted, too. A navvy will cry the easiest thing as is. If you'd only talk a little good to him you can make a navvy burst out crying like a child in a few minutes, if only you'd take him the right way.' Nevertheless they had come not because of their tender hearts but rather because of their pockets. Some were probably farm labourers who had left the villages in search of work and now here they were working the land again. Pickmen and shovellers were paid between 22s 6d and 24s a week, more than twice as much as on the farms. They owed their good fortune to a young man who would go on to become one of the greatest engineers the world has ever known – Isambard Kingdom Brunel.

There is a black-and-white photograph of Brunel taken some twenty years later against a backdrop of massive chain links. Black stove-pipe hat, cigar stuck between his teeth, loosely fitting three-quarter-length jacket, fob watch on the end of a chain fastened to a crumpled waistcoat, mud-splattered trousers and boots – an immediately recognisable image, a Victorian icon. The mud is surprising because at the time the photograph was taken he was one of the most celebrated engineers of his day and yet here he is in a shipyard looking like a contractor, or a foreman, but certainly not like one of the most famous men in England. But then it was the mud which had made him. He commissioned a travelling coach large enough for a bed, a drawing board and instruments, plans and a large cigar case, and set off to build a railway. He contracted workers and negotiated with landowners, possibly with Lamorock, although sadly no records survive.

He had been commissioned to build what was then the longest railway in the world, and, amazingly, he had no experience of designing railways. But then hardly anyone had. His entire railway experience had been one return trip on the Liverpool and Manchester some five years earlier, a trip on which he had taken his notebook and had written: 'I record this specimen of the shaking of the Manchester Railway. The time is not far off when we shall be able to take our coffee and write noiselessly and smoothly at 45 mph. Let me try.'

The pressure of work was intense: he told his senior assistant, 'it is harder work than I like. I am rarely much under twenty hours a day at it.' He rode and surveyed every inch of the line, checking every detail, and wrote to his directors giving them regular updates on the progress.

To the Directors of the Great Western Railway Company
18 Duke Street, Westminster
June 18th 1836

Gentlemen
. . . The cutting and embankment of the West End of
Tunnel No. 1 'Saltford' is however proceeding with about
200ft of the embankment being formed . . . the foundations
of an accommodation bridge in the meadows are in progress
and the bridge itself will be completed as soon as a larger
supply of stone can be brought from the quarry.
I am Gentlemen
Your most obt. St.
I K Brunel

The embankment and tunnel ran on the western perimeter of the
large field, visible from William's window, and the bridge in the
meadows crosses the road which now runs alongside the Shallows.
Brunel was a man who went through life with mud on his boots.

The work on the track was slow and it was not until the summer
of 1840, some three years after Queen Victoria had been crowned,
that gangs of extra men were contracted to work in relays seven
days a week, twenty-four hours per day, in one final push to get the
line open. And then on Monday, 31 August, a few minutes after 8
a.m. an engine called *Fire Ball* pulled away from the unfinished
Temple Meads station, the last rail laid in position only half an
hour earlier. The engine, gaily decorated with flags, pulled three
first-class carriages and five second-class carriages filled with members of the public who had obtained 'check tickets' in the large
booking hall. The passengers, though much excited by the adventure and the 'shouts of the multitude which lined the road', seem to
have behaved well – no one is known to have jumped off after his
hat, a not unusual occurrence in those days.

And then, about twenty minutes after the train left Bristol, smoke
was spotted by an eagle-eyed boy who had shinned up one of the
oaks on the banks of the river, the church bells began to peal, and *Fire
Ball* with her eight freshly painted carriages chock-full of nervous

passengers clasping smelling salts and hip flasks disappeared under the High Street. It was considered to be a dangerous business, this getting on a railway, so dangerous that the magazine *Punch* suggested that passengers should carry a 'Railway Pocket Companion, containing a small bottle of water, a tumbler, a complete set of surgical instruments, a packet of lint, and directions for making a will'. Nevertheless, the whole party emerged from the Saltford tunnel quite unscathed and ripped along the embankment which followed the river cheered on by the villagers who had rowed out to get a better view. The passengers arrived safe and sound at Bath station, also unfinished, some thirty-three minutes after leaving Bristol.

The country was now on the move. In 1842, some two years after the first train had rolled through Saltford, 24.5 million passengers travelled by train; by 1875 the figure had climbed to over 500 million. And yet the most mobile society in the world was also attached to its idea of the countryside, the village dream. Within every early Victorian town there were green spaces, parks with ponds and meadows, micro versions of the real thing. The railway companies gave their employees allotments beside the tracks where they could grow vegetables and flowers, a reminder perhaps of what they had lost.

James Austen, Jane's much loved elder brother, writing some years earlier, would have been amongst those who welcomed the transformation of the countryside. 'For in spite of all the fine things which Poets, both ancient and modern, have said on the charms of Solitude, and the happiness of a Country Life, an impartial examination of the matter will convince us that a dirty Village is not half as good a place to lounge in as the High Street, and that boarding at a Farmhouse is by no means so pleasant as dining at the Cross, the Star or the Angel.' James, who was at Oxford preparing for ordination in the Church of England, noticed many of his fellow students take a turn for the worse. 'So numerous, indeed, were the black coats, and so dismal the looks of the wearers, that I was almost led to imagine that there must be general mourning.' Closer observation revealed that these coats were worn by men who were about to ride off into a country sunset, never to be heard of again. It was a fate which James Austen feared might be his own and one which was beginning to feel more and more like mine. After all, who in their right mind would exchange life in London – one of the greatest cities in the world – for the solitude of a forgotten place in the country where all the exciting things had happened hundreds of years ago?

I picked my way down the High Street through freshly laid tractor treads of mud one Saturday morning, wondering how we had ended up in such a place. What kept me here was not my love of the countryside, my love of history, my love for Anna and the girls, wonderful though all these sound, especially when written after the event. No, it was a bull-headed desire to complete the building and live in it.

# 16

# Home Sweet Home

S AMUEL JOHNSON, the great sage of a previous era, could
have been speaking for me when he said, 'There is nothing,
Sir, too little for so little a creature as man. It is by studying
little things that we attain the great art of having as little misery
and as much happiness as possible.'

This is a story of little things – like the coin that Mark found
when plastering what was originally Lamorock's larder. It was a
penny dated 1862, wafer-thin, almost completely smooth . . .
until angled to catch the light, when slowly the profile of a young
woman emerged . . . Queen Victoria some twenty-five years into
her reign. When she had come to the throne the railways covered
a few hundred miles but by the end of her reign they ran not just
across the country but around the whole world, changing trans-
port for ever. Communications changed too. The electric telegraph, initially using the railway stations as sending and receiving
posts, allowed messages to be sent along wire. The Queen, particularly taken with this new method of communication, had her
own system set up in Buckingham Palace and delighted in sending messages along cables which had been laid across the Atlantic
and overland to India. The Great Western Railway was followed
by the Great Exhibition which was followed, rather less wonderfully, by the Great Stink – the name given to the appalling smell
which emerged from London's sewers during the long hot summer of 1858.

But it was not just the commercial and industrial worlds that
were changing. It was the Victorians who invented package holi-
days, ice creams and seaside piers, and they did so with all the
characteristic energy of their age. The writer George Eliot (a woman

who felt it necessary to use a man's name) complained that 'Even idleness is eager now – eager for amusement; prone to excursion-trains, art museums, periodical literature, and exciting novels'. With all this breathless activity it was not surprising that they needed some time to rest, a sort of no-go area between business and family. It was the Victorians who dreamed up the weekend, arguably one of their best ideas. And thus it was that the house, the place to which we all return at the end of the day when we've finished sending messages to India or building sewers, became increasingly important.

In 1861 Mrs Beeton published her hugely influential *Book of Household Management*, which began with these words: 'As with the COMMANDER OF AN ARMY, or the leader of any enterprise, so it is with the mistress of the house.' And there in one grand nine-teenth-century sentence you have it – running a house, like every-thing else, was now a professional matter.

Mrs Beeton had raised the bar. From this moment on, women felt there were new standards, new expectations. No longer was it enough to do what they could or even what was needed – looking after the house was now almost a spiritual matter. It is easy to see her words leading, in the end, to Nigella Lawson's hugely popular *How to Be a Domestic Goddess* (2001). It was Mrs Beeton who invented the idea of the domestic goddess. Here she is again: 'I have always thought there is no more fruitful source of family dis-content than a housewife's badly-cooked dinners and untidy ways. Men are now so well served out of doors – at their clubs, well-ordered taverns, and dining-houses, that in order to compete with the attractions of these places, a mistress must be thoroughly acquainted with the theory and practice of cookery, as well as be perfectly conversant with the other arts of making and keeping a comfortable home.' And so it was that Jane Austen's giggling hero-ines were upstaged by regiments of wives determined to turn their houses into homes, domestic sanctuaries where their husbands could rest their brows . . . or so the story went. But not in Saltford – Lamorock and Thomas never married and 'the mistress of the house', assumed by Mrs Beeton to be a dutiful wife, was in fact a housekeeper called Rachel Weymouth.

Family was a Victorian buzzword; there were Family Butchers, Family Drapers and new magazines with titles like *Family Economist*, *Family Friend*, *Family Treasure* and *Family Prize Magazine*, as if friends, treasures and prizes could only be found within families. There are two bachelors in *Our Mutual Friend* by Charles Dickens who take some rooms together; one of them wants what he calls a 'very complete little kitchen', because of its potential to change his character, to bring him closer, perhaps, to being married. 'The moral influence is the thing . . . See! . . . miniature flour barrel, rolling pin, spice box, shelf of brown jars, chopping board, coffee-mill, dresser elegantly furnished with crockery, saucepans and pans, roasting jack, a charming kettle, an armoury of dish-covers . . .' – kitchen utensils with moral influence! In Mrs Beeton's book a roasting-jack made a cameo appearance, held over the fire by a version of the huge agricultural-looking contraption which was hanging next to the fireplace in our nearly completed kitchen. Many people thought  that meat roasted in one of the new oven ranges was less good than that cooked over an open fire, and this device meant that the meat could be cooked evenly. An old coin, a kitchen gadget; props left by people who, it now seemed to me, had just popped out a few moments earlier.

Men who lived outside of families were considered only to have half-lives and were often pictured living in lodgings, pressed against furniture by lusty landladies – women who did for cash what decent women gave for free. Such men lived outside of what the Victorians called 'an establishment', which was not of course the situation of Lamorock and Thomas. Saltford was not just *an* establishment, it was *the* establishment. Nevertheless there were probably those in the village who wondered, in the way that only villages can, whether Rachel Weymouth was quite *nice*.

There is a fascinating entry in the private journal of one of the great men of the age, written when he was considering marriage to a girl called Mary. He does what advice-givers down the ages have recommended: he draws a line down the middle of the paper and lists the pros and cons.

| MARRY | NOT MARRY |
|---|---|
| Children – (if it Please God) – Constant companion & friend in old age) who will feel interested in one, – object *to be beloved* and played with. Better than a dog anyhow. – Home, & someone to take Care of house – Charms of music & female chit-chat. – These things good for one's health. – *but terrible loss of time*. – My God, it is intolerable To Think of spending ones whole life, like a neuter bee, working, working, & nothing after all. No, no won't do. Imagine living all one's day solitary in smoky dirty London House. – Only picture to Yourself a nice soft wife on a sofa with a good fire, & books and music perhaps Compare this vision with the dingy reality of Grt. Marlbro' St. | Freedom to go where one liked – choice of Society *little of it*. Conversation of clever men at clubs – Not forced to visit relatives, & to bend in every trifle. – to have the expense & anxiety of children – perhaps quarrelling **Loss of time**. – cannot read in the Evenings – fatness & idleness – Anxiety & responsibility less money for books &c – if many children forced to gain one's bread. But then it is very bad for ones health to work too much. Perhaps my wife wont like London; then the sentence is banishment & degradation into indolent, idle fool. |

Marry – Mary – Marry Q.E.D.

So ran the private thoughts of Charles Darwin, celebrated for his theory of evolution, man descended from apes and all that. And he was not alone. The father of another great thinker, John Ruskin, expressed similar feelings. 'Oh! How dull and dreary is the best society I fall into compared with the circle of my own Fire Side with my Love sitting opposite irradiating all around her, and my most extraordinary boy.'

This was the Victorian ideal, families gathered around a fire-side; a similar image to a drawing showing not one but two extraordinary boys. It was created by E.H. Shepard (the illustrator of Winnie the Pooh), who remembered his Victorian childhood well. The drawing shows him and his brother safely tucked away in front of the fire. It feels like a winter's afternoon at Saltford; curtains drawn moments earlier by the housekeeper, the sound of rain on glass. But the fireplace here is not just impressive, it's majestic, framed by beautifully fluted stone columns spanned by an oak mantelpiece with echoes of a medieval church; more St John than John Lewis.

In 1864 (the year that John Lewis first opened its doors to the public), George Alexander Flower, Lamorock's nephew and the closest thing he had to an 'extraordinary boy', was seven years old. Children were bundled up under endless layers of clothing and the boys in this picture, sitting in front of a roasting fire, were probably less comfortable than they looked. Real seven-year-old boys, even ones with haircuts and clothes like those in E.H. Shepard's drawing, cannot just sit and be good. When he came to Saltford, George Alexander would have been down at the Shallows fishing, mucking around on the farm, drifting in and out of the kitchen. 'In December,' continued Mrs Beeton, 'the principal household duty lies in preparing for the creature comforts of those near and dear to us, so as to meet old Christmas with a happy face, a contented mind, and a full larder; and in stoning plums, washing currants, cutting the citron, beating the eggs, and *mixing the pudding* . . .' Licking *that* bowl would have been fun.

Mrs Beeton's book was illustrated with colour engravings on almost every page and was the first to set out recipes in the format still used today. Food was the way a woman kept her man at home and was therefore important; a view shared by the two million people who bought her book when it first came out, one of whom might very well have been Rachel Weymouth. Mrs B's suggestions were characteristically Victorian, she had no time for the extravagance of earlier times. Here, for example, are some of her dinner recommendations for a comfortable middle-class household, a household not unlike the one under Rachel.

THURSDAY
Pea Soup made from liquor that beef was boiled in. Cold Beef. Mashed Potatoes. Mutton Cutlets and Tomato sauce. Macaroni.

FRIDAY
Bubble and Squeak, made from remains of cold beef. Roast
Shoulder of Veal, stuffed, and spinach and potatoes. Boiled
Batter Pudding and Sweet Sauce.

SATURDAY
Stewed Veal and Vegetables, made from remains of the shoulder.
Broiled rumpsteaks and oyster sauce. Yeast Dumplings.

Chances are Lamorock and Thomas were not skinny. Chances are
too that their food had been boiled beyond the point of useful life.
Take for example her Thursday suggestions. She recommended
boiling macaroni for between one and a half and one and three-
quarters of an hour, cutlets needed two hours, as did rice and large
carrots.

If the major battle was fought in the kitchen, the other battle, in
which only short-term victories could ever be achieved, was in the
arena of dirt. And dirt, for the Victorians, was a big deal. The orna-
ments and clocks in E.H. Shephard's drawing were covered in glass
to protect them from the soot and dirt produced by the fire below.
This was the 'dust' which dustmen would collect, though there was
no need for dustmen here as soot and ash went back on the land as
fertiliser – but with five fires it was a difficult house to keep clean,
still is. Door latches had small plates or curtains fitted over the key-
hole to keep out dirt; plants were kept on windowsills to trap air-
borne dirt as it crept in through the gaps around the windows; and
tablecloths were laid at the last minute, in order to try to keep
them clean a little longer.

Towards the end of the century a new range of soaps became
available. Until then soap was sold in long bars by grocers, who cut
off a portion with a wire, rather like cheese, selling it by weight.
This is an advertisement for one of the new penny packets of soap,
snappily entitled: 'A FRIENDLY BIT OF CHIT-CHAT BETWEEN
MRS. SCRUBWELL AND MRS. THRIFTY'.

SCRUBWELL: Good morning, Neighbour Thrifty. How are
you and your family? But how is this? I understood that
you had your week's wash today, and I expected to find you

'up to the elbows' in suds; instead of which, here is a clean dry house, and the dinner table all in apple pie order, ready for your husband on his coming home from work. Are you going to put off your wash till next week?

THRIFTY: Why neighbour, *I have done my washing!* I began at a little before 9 o'clock this morning, have washed every rag of clothes, and look, they are on the lines in the garden, nearly dry.

SCRUBWELL: Well, I *am* surprised. But do you mean to say that you have washed all that lot of clothes this morning. *Impossible, surely!*

THRIFTY: Impossible or not, *it is quite true* . . .

SCRUBWELL: You amaze me neighbour. How have you done it, and who have you had to help you?

THRIFTY: Oh, it is easy enough to get rid of the slap-dash, stem, and dribbling-slops on a wash day, in good time. I can always make quick work of *my* washing by using Harper Twelvetrees' 'Glycerine Soap-Powder', and it makes the clothes beautifully clean and white too, I assure you. I scarcely ever rub our clothes now, and you know how black my Jim's shirts get at the Foundry.

SCRUBWELL: But how do you get the clothes clean if you do not rub them well?

THRIFTY: I mean that I don't often find it necessary to rub them after I take them out of the soaking water. Of course, I always soak the white clothes over night, and soap the collars and wristbands of shirts, and rub the part most soiled; but I don't stand rubbing the clothes to pieces, and rubbing the skin off my hands at the wash-tub all the next day, as some people do.

SCRUBWELL: Well, this is wonderful! I had no idea that washing day could be got over with so little trouble and labour. I think I shall try this wonderful powder.

THRIFTY: If you give it a *fair trial*, you will find even greater advantages than quickly getting the clothes out of the way. For instance, my husband, though a good, quiet, sober man (a teetotaller) used to be sadly out of the way on washing days; for our house you know is small and we have no wash house. But he knows very little about the wash, except the pleasure of having clean linen when he requires it.

SCRUBWELL: That's capital! I'll certainly try Harper Twelvetrees' 'Glycerine' at once, for my husband has often been sadly out of temper on washing-days, and has frequently gone to the public-house, because, he said, he had no comfort at home.

THRIFTY: And just consider what you save, in time, trouble, and labour, by using this 'Glycerine Soap-powder.' Just consider the difference between slop, slop, slopping about all day, and having your house cleaned up before dinner, or nearly so . . .

(Enter James Thrifty, smiling at his nice clean house, and well-spread dinner table.)

They were talking about washing for heaven's sake! But that perhaps was the point, they were, in a sense, washing for heaven's sake – it was a world stiff with morality, a world in which even adverts for washing powder sounded like sermons.

Now, in the closing decades of the century, Saltford was on the skids, and the future was in James Thrifty's foundry not on Lamorock Flower's farm. Yeoman farmers were a dying breed, as they had been for over a hundred years, but now they disappeared almost completely. Farming went through one of its periodic slumps; grain supplies from the American prairies flooded the home markets and many farmers went bankrupt. Salford had not been able to take advantage of the new farming methods of the previous century, hampered as it was by ancient agreements with the dozens of smallholders, which meant that as the nineteenth century progressed it got left further and further behind.

Some fifty years earlier William Cobbett, in his revolutionary broadsheet, had written about a new breed of money men, 'bull-frogs' who gobbled down the small tenant farmers in one gulp. He harked back to earlier times when '*You*, the *bull-frogery*, did not flourish indeed; for, as yet, you were not! It was the paper-money that created you. It was that; it was the false capital; it was the moulding of a dozen farms into one; it was the making of simple men and small farmers mere labourers; it was that that made you flourish, while those who did the work were perishing.' The pity was that Lamorock had not been a bull-frog; had he been, Saltford might well have been in better shape. A parish plan dated 1851 shows that there were 410 separate parcels of land with 50 different owners. The land pattern was much as it had been in the late Middle Ages: small plots scattered around the village which were held by lifelong tenants at fixed rents. Lamorock recognised the time had come for a change: he rented out the land but continued to live in the house and then, in 1879, he died.

The bequests in his will, copies of which still exist, were predictable – the freehold of Saltford went to George Alexander Flower and Rachel got a small annuity. The more interesting information was the inclusion of two other names; one had made a cameo appearance some fifty years earlier and the other was about to become a main player, albeit an unlikely one.

Lamorock had appointed the Reverend Charles Edward Leopold Wightman of Shrewsbury in the County of Salop Clerk as trustee and executor. The man who had attended the tree-planting ceremony in the churchyard some fifty years earlier, son of the rector under whom Lamorock had served as churchwarden, was still a part of Lamorock's life. The fact that he was still in touch with Charles, especially as he was now living in Shrewsbury, suggested, at the very least, that Lamorock was a man who knew about friendship – you don't keep friends for fifty years by accident. Lamorock's friendship with Charles had been forged in the early years of their lives. Things often happen between people that nothing can ever undo, no matter that the two parties sometimes see little of each other in later life. That he never married may well have made this friendship all the more important. In any event Lamorock appears to have built his own personalised circle, not a family in the strict Victorian sense of the word, but something closer to what today we would call a network – Rachel, George Alexander Flower and Charles Wightman – all people to whom he had felt close.

A good death was one in which the dying person had time to tie up all the loose ends in spiritual and worldly terms. On the available evidence, namely his will and the subsequent events surrounding the house, Lamorock appears to have died well; quite possibly with George Alexander and Rachel saying their final farewells and Charles Wightman praying at his bedside. As soon as the final moment had passed, Rachel went around the house closing the blinds, which were not opened again until after the funeral.

Letters were written, perhaps by George Alexander, on black-edged paper, sent in envelopes with black borders, whose thickness showed the importance of his relationship with the deceased. If the death was sudden and the recipient elderly then he would have been expected to write on plain unmarked paper in order to avoid causing too big a shock. That the will had been drawn up just a few months beforehand suggested that his death was no surprise, indeed it suggested that he had timed it well.

And then there was the funeral itself and the vexing issue of who should be invited. Women, so the argument went, should stay away because of their inability to contain their emotions. It was a view which had many supporters – Queen Victoria had not attended her beloved Albert's funeral.

Victoria wrote to her eldest daughter, 'How am I, who leant on him for all and everything – without whom I did nothing, moved not a finger, arranged not a print or photograph, didn't put on a gown or bonnet if he didn't approve it shall go on, to live, to move, to help myself in difficult moments?' She wore black for the rest of her life and for the next twenty years mourning clothes (who should wear what and for how long) were the subject of much discussion. As ever, how things looked was the key. Curiously, the period of mourning was decided not by personal feeling but by a socially approved timetable of grief. A husband warranted two to three years, a wife three months, a parent or a child one year, aunts and uncles three months, first cousins four to six weeks. Peter Robinson's, a London store, opened a special branch called Black Peter Robinson's to mark it out from the original branch which sold normal clothes for normal life. So precise were the different gradations of clothes available that this new branch had within it something called a 'Mitigated Affliction Department' which dealt exclusively in clothes for half-mourning, the least severe of all the stages, coming as it did after first, second and ordinary mourning.

Versions of the following fictitious conversation, written some years earlier, may perhaps have been heard in Peter Robinson's:

> LADY: And as to the change of dress. Sir; I suppose you will have a great variety of half-mourning?
>
> SHOPMAN: Oh! Infinite – the largest in town. Full, and half, and quarter, and half-quarter, shaded off, if I may say so, like an India-ink drawing, from a grief *pronounce* to the slightest *nuance* of regret.

But in the country everything was rather simpler; simpler and cheaper. If women did attend the ceremony in St Mary's church they were more likely to be wearing clothes they had been given or lent or possibly an everyday dress dyed black, the cheapest solution of all.

The ceremony would also have been simple, certainly compared with the elaborate affairs that regularly took place in Bath and Bristol. For a start the church was next door, so no need for a carriage and horse – the coffin could be carried from the house into the church in a couple of minutes. Nevertheless clothes were a way of showing community solidarity: a black dress however simple for women and a black armband for men however rough was a way of being included, a sort of tribal connection. There were few in St Mary's churchyard that day born before Lamorock; he had been a churchwarden for half a lifetime, was respected by most and loved by some. Ashes to ashes, dust to dust . . . the coffin was lowered into the ground and the crowd shuffled back down the village green, heading for their homes, apart from one man who stood looking back towards the house.

Charles Brimble was an entrepreneur; some ten years earlier the beginnings of the Midland Railway Branch line had appeared at the bottom of his garden and he had turned his cottage into an inn to meet the demands of the large number of navvies working on the new line. And now here he was leaving Lamorock's funeral about to move into the dead man's house. Flushed with cash from his new enterprise, Charles had done another deal and got the old man to rent him the house, so in fact he had been farming the land for the last year. An odd thing that a house once blessed by a bishop and designed by a prince was about to be owned by the village publican, but there it was in the records.

And there it still is, a couple of hundred metres down the High Street – The Bird, more properly The Bird in Hand – the place where Steve and I met to discuss lighting. Two large pieces of paper held down by empty beer glasses and ashtrays were spread across two tables.

'I'm just wondering about the kitchen – do you think twenty-four halogen are enough?'

'It depends.'

'On what?'

'On how bright you want it.'

'I want it bright.'

'You got it – it's massive – you'll need a sub-station for that lot.'

'Fine . . . but I don't want it to look sterile – like some sort of laboratory – know what I mean?'

'Not really.'

'It's a kitchen, so I want it to be welcoming, nurturing – you know, yellow, which is why I've gone for all these tungsten tubes in the alcoves under the plate rack and cupboards – to warm it up.'

'You can't expect them to do that – that's Dave's department.' Dave was the plumber in charge of the central heating.

'No, I mean warm as in look.'

'James, you tell me where to put them and I'll do it. OK?'

A couple more drinks, the conversation meandering nowhere in particular. It was, I think, Steve who brought us back on line.

'What about outside?'

'What about it?' Outside lighting was not something I had considered.

'You could do something really good.'

'Nice one . . . like what?'

'I was thinking a couple of floods over here at the end of the lawn.'

'OK – to light up the trees?'

'No – to light up the house.'

'What? – no, we don't want that.'

'You can get really good ones – mini versions of what they use at football grounds.'

'Anna would hate it – well, so would I actually.'

'Why?'

'We don't want everyone seeing the house, that's one of the great things about it – it's tucked away so no one *can* see it.'

'Up to you – if you can't afford it fair enough but you should put the cables in – might change your mind later.'

A few days later in answer to one of Steve's questions about cables in the drawing room I recall asking another question.

'What do people usually have?'

'People don't *usually* live in houses like this.'

# · 17 ·

# Changing Times

SALTFORD TIME WAS nine or ten minutes behind London time – being further west it saw the sunrise later. This wasn't significant when estimates for journeys were measured in fractions of a day but now everything was *so* precise; ten minutes was the difference between catching and missing a train.

In the absence of a proper station, the Midland Railway Company asked the new landlord of The Bird in Hand for permission to fix a timetable to the wall – 6.49, 7.39, 8.49, 11.19, 12.52 . . . time was measured out, minutely scheduled and eventually even saved. It was possible, perhaps, to see the railway era marking the moment at which time lost its rhythm: a blurring of the natural divisions between labour and holiday, winter and spring, even night and day. When the employee of the Midland Railway Company fixed his timetable to the Bird in Hand he was ushering in a timescale increasingly referred to as 'railway time'. From now on the guard would use his watch to check the time at each station and soon it was the station clock and not the church bell – the corporate employee and not the vicar – who set the time.

In the period between seeing Saltford and exchanging contracts, I spoke, amongst others, to the then landlord of The Bird in Hand, the owners of the newsagent, anyone really, trying to find out as much as I could about the house. I was struck by how significant the house was in the minds of those I talked to; it was the house, not us, that was of interest. And so it proved to be: for the first few years the house went before us. Our identities are often wrapped up, it seemed to me, as much in where we live as in what we do. How we organise our living space, how big it is, what we put on the walls – all speak volumes about what kinds of people we are, or at least how we wish others to see us. And so it was with the Victorians – but with one big difference: our concern is with property ownership, theirs was with occupancy and display. Only about 10 per cent of Victorians owned their houses; the rest rented. The poorest paid by the week and the prosperous middle classes, a rank Charles Brimble had just entered, took renewable seven-year leases. Charles moved in for Christmas – lucky man – and probably found like the rest of us that Saltford appeared to have been made with Christmas in mind.

Eleven years later  Kodak had produced a camera which used glass plates and paper 'film', Charlie Chaplin had been born in London, and an unknown photographer stood in the garden at Saltford and took a photograph of the back of the house dated 1890.

So here, wonderfully, was the north face as it stood in the closing decade of the nineteenth century. William's window, set between two supporting buttresses, the weathered old lion just visible on the east gable of the main house, the same dusky clay tiles on the roof (Romans on the steep slopes of the main house and pantiles elsewhere), but best by far, the small wing with a walled-up door, crowned by a cross, thought to have started life as an Elizabethan chapel. This was the building which, extraordinarily, was later allowed to fall down. And just visible, if you look very carefully, cutting across the lower right-hand corner of the frame are a few more pantiles, the edge of another building long since vanished.

The dusky sleepiness of this photograph is perhaps significant; the Manor's position in the pecking order of village houses had changed in the course of the last hundred years. It had always been uncontested, standing head and shoulders above the surrounding cottages and small farms, unquestionably *the* house of the village, but now there was Saltford House whose inhabitants did not depend for their wealth on the land or what it produced. Many of these newcomers were retired army and naval officers, attracted by the railways and the ease of access to Bath. Typical of this new breed was Admiral Kelly, whose house was crammed with books on the discoveries in New Guinea, steamships, geometry and trigonometry, dictionaries in four languages, *Burke's Peerage and Gentry*, Gisborne's *An Enquiry into the Duties of the Female Sex*. It was the Admiral's wife, Mrs Kelly, not the publican's wife, who gave woollen cloaks to the girls in the village school – which, incidentally, she had completely rebuilt in 1874 – and organised the distribution of coal and soup to the poor. Her house had two vineries and a tomato house – frivolities not to be seen in the photograph of Saltford.

Mrs Kelly was followed by another of her kind, a Colonel Rolleston, a bluff ex-army man who had spent many years in South Africa under the command of Lord Roberts (or Bobs as he was called by his soldiers). In October 1899 the British-occupied town of Mafeking was under siege and its success in surviving the longest siege of the war (217 days) was attributed to the plucky resolve of its commander, Robert Baden-Powell. He had succeeded with style – dummy minefields, bogus orders shouted through a makeshift megaphone, make-believe barbed wire (which men mimed stepping through) and Sunday baby competitions – so very English, the same mixture of grit and imagination which he would fashion into the worldwide Scouting Movement. Near the end of the siege Baden-Powell had been asked if he would consider playing cricket with the Afrikaners. The reply came that he had to first finish the present game, the protracted siege, which so far had lasted '200 days, not out'. Baden-Powell had become an imperial symbol, the hero of an empire under threat, and his name would surely have been on the lips of most men in Saltford on the night that Colonel Rolleston bought them all a pint of beer to celebrate the breaking of the siege.

Queen Victoria died in 1901. She had reigned for sixty-three years, longer than any other English monarch. The country's industries had continued to grow during the closing decade of her reign but at nothing like the earlier rate of expansion. Those who were looking ahead had begun to see her not as the head of an empire on which the sun never set, but rather as the figurehead of a lost civilisation. The time was ripe for a change but the hands to which the country had been bequeathed were less than ideal, belonging to a sixty-year-old man whom the writer Henry James called 'Edward . . . fat Edward . . . Edward the Caresser'. Confessor to Caresser in nine hundred years: he had a point. Edward VII was known to be a womaniser, a roly-poly figure smoking cigars and shuffling lecherously about from one house party to another. On the day Victoria's death was announced, *The Times* thundered its disapproval of a man who in his youth had 'been importuned by temptation in its most seductive forms' and who must surely have prayed 'lead us not into temptation [with] a feeling akin to hopelessness'.

Nevertheless, the century of the common man had begun. A hundred thousand football fans watched the 1901 Cup Final at Crystal Palace, Mrs Pankhurst was warming up to lead the charge for women's votes; and in the words of W.B. Yeats, 'Everybody got down off their stilts'. He should perhaps have qualified his remark by saying everybody lucky enough to have stilts, which did not include women. When Edward came to the throne there were 172,000 women teachers, 64,000 women nurses, but only 6 architects, 3 vets, 2 accountants and no solicitors or barristers. Nor did it include the majority of people living in Saltford. In 1902 an Education Act was passed to improve both the government 'maintained' schools and the 'voluntary' church schools of the kind that villages like Saltford, with a well-established church presence, had had for years. Every child was to have the right to a basic education and every year almost everything that happened was an improvement on the year before. No longer would children be released from their desks to work in the field. From now on school would be compulsory.

Perhaps that accounts for some of the serious faces at Queen's School, so called because the building stood in Queen's Square. The photograph was taken just a few metres from our recently restored lamps and seemed oddly familiar; different costumes from the school photos in our girls' bedrooms but the same faces. Take for example Clifford Brown, sitting, although only just, on the far left of the fourth row. Clearly he only had a small bit of the bench – perhaps the photographer had decided to put him next to the girls at the last minute and May Harding, one of the most confident girls in the school, was reluctant to shift up. Look carefully and it seems her hand may have been giving him a discreet push. At the back, just next to kind-looking Miss Slade, is W.H.A. Trimby, the boy with the flower in his buttonhole. His father was Colonel Rolleston's gardener and he went on to spend his life growing plants, something which his son, who lives in the same house over-looking the churchyard, continues to do. Further along the same row stood Ada Weymouth and Beatrice Brimble and below them Elsie Brimble and what looks like Ada's younger brother. No longer were the Manor children and their friends sent away to school or educated by tutors, as they had been for hundreds of years. They muddled along with everyone else at the village school.

But there was another photograph, this time of Rachel Weymouth's husband, Frederick James, the village coal and timber merchant between 1860 and 1902. A squat, bearded figure, hold-ing a pony and cart, described elsewhere as 'small in stature', so small that whenever he went down to the Bird his fellow drinkers would sit him up on the counter for his drink. At some point, pos-sibly with Rachel's encouragement after she had finished working up at the Manor, he began to collect washing from houses around the village, taking it into Bath to be professionally laundered. The cost of washing was substantial, so substantial that when people stayed with friends they expected to be presented with their wash-ing bill on departure. A household that spent £25 per year on rent might expect to pay between £6 and £10 per year on laundry. But sending laundry out, though cheaper than hiring women to come to the house, was not without its anxieties. There was always the risk of what one doctor called the 'promiscuous' mixing of his laun-dry with unknown others. Whitley's department store in London had opened a laundry section – a venture which flopped until it began to separate each household's laundry, indicating this segrega-tion by returning the servants' laundry in different-coloured wrap-ping paper. A sensible householder instructed that everything be unpacked downstairs, hanging it before the fire to air, thus ensuring that if bugs did jump from one item to another they did so in the servants' quarters.

In 1908 Robert Baden-Powell, one of Colonel Rolleston's great favourites, published *Scouting for Boys*, a rag-bag of a book which contained anecdotes, campfire yarns, first-aid tips and advice on observation and tracking. Not, you might think, an obvious best-seller. You'd be wrong. It was printed by the owner of the *Daily Express* in a six-part serialisation in the tried and tested formula of the *Boy's Own Paper* and was an immediate success. Between 1908 and 1945 the only English book to exceed its sales was the Bible. *Scouting for Boys* sent ripples around the world and would in due course prove to be significant for Saltford.

The image of a sunny summer's afternoon is often used to describe the spirit of Edwardian England. Buttered scones, yellow cream and home-made jam, unclouded blue skies – like one of those films with Helena Bonham Carter surrounded by floppy men with floppy hair. Perhaps the closest that Saltford got to this society world (and it wasn't very close) was the annual regatta held down at the Shallows and referred to by the local newspaper as 'the Henley of the West'. It reported, 'Sunshine at the Salford regatta has become an almost unknown quantity and the dull morning that greeted the waking eyes of the West of England was in keeping with the experience of the recent years.' It said that the run of bad luck which had provided a wet day for the previous twelve years had been broken . . . a storm which had appeared imminent held off. But not for long.

The country went to war with Germany on the night of 4 August 1914, having received no reply to her ultimatum that invading German troops must be recalled from Belgium. This new war was very different from any that had gone before. The Crimean War, the Boer War and the fighting in India had been distant affairs carried out by professional soldiers, men like Admiral Kelly and Colonel Rolleston, whose rooms were full of tigers' tusks and medals. This was far more serious. For a start it was closer, being just across the Channel, and secondly it required the participation of ordinary men. Very soon Kitchener was staring down the barrel of his arm, pointing his finger at the men of Saltford and telling them, should they be in any doubt, that their country needed them. Behind Kitchener stood God, the King and something which Baden-Powell had spoken of some years earlier: the spirit of the games pitch – cricket for the officers and football for the other ranks – and all this combined with nostalgia for the old days of Empire. The desire to serve was intense. At Cheltenham College, the language school, whose options included Sanskrit and Hindustani, was housed in a bigger building than the Classics department. But Kitchener's call to arms was addressed to Englishmen, no matter whether they attended Cheltenham College or Queen's School, played cricket or football. It offered a real-life boys'-own adventure which most thought would be over by Christmas. This, then, was the spirit of 1914 and the spirit that walked into Queen's School, now a temporary recruiting centre. Men, many of whom had sat in the same room only months before, shook hands with those already in uniform, eager to have a go at the Hun.

Early one morning the village gathered to watch the first enlisted men assemble in Queen's Square. The sergeant major shuffled his new recruits into something that looked passably like a company of soldiers, the small band struck up and the whole body wheeled around the corner and up the High Street, across which a banner had been hung – 'Good Luck Lads'.

In many villages, and Saltford appears to have been one of them, life jogged on without appearing to change. Some words written on Christmas Eve 1914 about an old house in Hampshire could just as easily have been written about Saltford:

> . . . I came down to the old manor farm,
> And church and yew-tree opposite, in age
> Its equals and in size. The church and yew
> And farmhouse slept in a Sunday silentness.
> The air raised not a straw. The steep farm roof,
> With tiles duskily glowing, entertained
> The mid-day sun; and up and down the roof
> White pigeons nestled . . .
> This England, Old already, was called Merry.

This England, the writer suggests, an England in which everything would remain the same for ever and ever, was a nostalgic dream. But Christmas is a time for nostalgia, especially when it snows. A private in the London Rifles woke up in the trenches on Christmas morning to find

> everything was covered in snow, everything was white. The devastated landscape looked terrible in its true colours – clay and mud and broken brick – but when it was covered in

snow, it was beautiful. Then we heard the Germans singing 'Silent night, Holy night', and they put up a notice saying 'Merry Christmas', so we put up one too. While they were singing our boys said, 'Let's join in,' so we joined in and when we started singing, they stopped. And when we stopped, they started again. So we were easing the way. Then one German took a chance and jumped up on top of the trench and shouted out, 'Happy Christmas, Tommy!' So of course our boys said, 'If he can do it, we can do it,' and we all jumped up. A sergeant-major shouted, 'Get down!' But we said, 'Shut up Sergeant, it's Christmas time!'

But something *had* changed. As the war dragged on, more and more homes in the village learnt that a son, brother or father had not come safely through. But it was not just homes that were affected. Former pupils on leave from France would return to visit their old school, to be fêted by the teachers and pupils. Young soldiers volunteered to collect a younger brother or sister and arrived a few moments early, the better to enjoy the role of conquering hero, especially if they brought a gas mask or an enemy helmet around which to spin a story. For many the classroom was a place where they would first hear the news. It was not uncommon to see the headmaster enter the class, cross to the teacher's desk, talk seriously for a moment and leave. A few moments later one of their number was walking home to a letter, *the* letter, saying his brother or father had been killed.

Five million Allied soldiers lost their lives in the Great War but figures like these, any figures, only tell a partial story. This is a son recalling the moment when he broke the news of his eldest brother's death to his father who was working in the fields:

I waited for him to finish a bout with his plough and two horses. 'George has been killed,' I told him. He stood for a moment. He didn't answer, didn't say a word, but left his horse all steaming in the early November weather and together we walked back in silence to the house. When we got home my father went to the bottom of the stairs and called up 'That's right, ain't it?' he made no attempt to go up and comfort my mother but went into the kitchen, sat in his wooden armchair and put his arms on the table and his head on his arms for a little while – wept for a few moments, I think. But that sticks in my memory, that he didn't go upstairs to comfort my mother.

Death came to rich and poor alike but the means of communication were different – letters for soldiers, telegrams for officers. Harry Lauder, a popular music-hall star, was one of those who received a telegram on New Year's Day 1917.

> I knew what it contained. God! The agonies I suffered that bright New Year's morning . . . hundreds of thousands, aye, millions of fathers and mothers will know just what I passed through for many hours and for many weeks. My only son. The one child God had given us.

Harry found a way to do something with his feelings. His son's last words were said to have been 'Carry on.' That afternoon Harry composed what is now perhaps his best-known song, a song he performed that evening.

> *Keep right on to the end of the road,*
> *Keep right on to the end,*
> *Tho' the way be long, let your heart be strong,*
> *Keep right on round the bend.*
> *Tho' you're tired and weary still journey on,*
> *Till you come to your happy abode,*
> *Where all the love you've been dreaming of*
> *Will be there at the end of the road.*

As the war entered its fourth year the outlook was bleak. Two-thirds of the country's food came from overseas, German U-boats were sinking increasingly large numbers of Allied merchant ships and enormous quantities of meat and grain ended up at the bottom of the sea. The House of Commons was told that the country's food supplies could run out in a matter of weeks. Most families were simply not getting enough food. What bread they did get was smeared with a thin veneer of margarine, the great wartime substitute for butter, which was now only to be found on the table of Colonel Rolleston and his kind.

This was a national crisis; but it was also personal. A woman at the end of her life, remembering her childhood in a village just across the county border, wrote:

> It was a terrible time, terrible. We were starving. I can remember my mother going out and picking dandelion leaves and washing them and making sandwiches with them . . . many days our mother would make a jug of custard for our dinner, and we ate it with bread and butter. Nothing else. I got sick of the sight of custard. I don't know how my mother managed. It was nothing to see her sitting at the table with an empty plate. 'Mummy, you're not eating?' 'I'm not hungry,' she'd say. Whatever she had was for my brother and myself. If it had gone on for many more months like that I don't know what would have happened to us.

Neither did the people of Saltford, which was why, on 7 January 1917, the Parish Council purchased a potato sprayer for £4 4s. It was a significant gesture. In February the German Admiralty calculated that their U-boats could sink 600,000 tons of Allied merchant shipping every month, which they calculated would bring the country to its knees within six months. The Kaiser pledged to 'starve the British people, until they, who have refused peace, will kneel and plead for it'. As the crisis worsened there must have been some who would happily have pleaded, the mother of this nine-year-old girl amongst them:

> We were very poverty-stricken. Really my baby brothers starved to death. There was no food for them. I can remember one kindly doctor coming to see them for nothing, no money, and he told my mother they had to have Virol every day. That was kind of a thick, sticky malt stuff. But, well, we didn't have pennies every day to give the babies. I remember when my last brother died, the one I used to look after. I think I looked on him as a doll, I never had a toy. Then one day they said he's died. When I went to bed at night his dead body was being kept in a coffin in my bedroom before being buried and my mother said, 'Say goodnight to him, won't you?' I did. I used to kiss him goodnight and he looked lovely. I did say to

my mother one night, 'He's ever so cold, shall I take him to bed with me?' And she said, 'No, you mustn't disturb him.' I used to feel sorry that he was on his own and I used to think, 'They're going to take him away.' To begin with, there was some bubbles of spittle at the corner of his mouth and I thought, 'Well, if he was ill, if I take those and put them in my mouth I'll probably die and go with him and so I can look after him again.' I missed him, missed his coughing when he'd gone. I remember the day he went. Someone gave my mother and grandma a lift because she sat in this pony-trap with this coffin in her lap.

Horticultural advisers from the government's Food Production Department urged schools and hospitals to turn over all available land to help feed the nation. King George V decreed that potatoes, cabbage and other vegetables should replace geraniums in the flower beds opposite Buckingham Palace. Prime Minister Lloyd George announced that he was growing King Edward potatoes. In April, Mr Snelgrove, one of the Ministry of Food's unsung heroes, visited Queen's School to discuss the conversion of a pasture, by the path leading to the church, into a kitchen garden where the children could grow vegetables in the national interest. The campaign was a huge success – by the end of the war there would be over 90,000 acres spread across the whole country under allotments, two of which were tended by the teachers and children from Queen's School.

On 11 November 1918 an armistice was declared. That day everybody was in the High Street singing, waving Union Jacks, dancing in the streets; people were overwhelmed with relief but for many the agony was not over. One prisoner of war, returning in December 1918, recalled seeing a woman walking along outside the train carriage in which he stood, holding up a picture of what he assumed to be her husband, in the hope that someone might have some information.

The decision to mark the first anniversary of the armistice with two minutes' silence was taken just a few weeks earlier. It was a decision which chimed perfectly with the mood of the country. Railway stations fell silent, telephone exchanges stopped putting through calls, buyers stopped buying and servers stopped serving. A writer for *The Times* described how he had been travelling on a bus with friends. In the minutes before the silence they had been 'discussing with a forced cynicism of which each of us was secretly ashamed, some supposedly humorous side of the proposed stand-still'. Just before eleven o'clock the bus pulled to a halt outside a small factory. The correspondent saw '10 or a dozen factory workers wearing overalls but not caps, standing rigidly to attention. Glancing along the road we saw at irregular intervals perhaps twenty people, mostly women . . . some with children in perambulators. Without exception they stood still . . . It was then that we four cynics . . . realized that we too were on our feet with our heads uncovered.' At the end of the silence the factory workers gave three cheers for victory and the four men on the bus, three of whom had been soldiers themselves, joined the cheering.

And so on Sunday, 14 November 1920, a year after the first anniversary, Saltford had what was reported as a 'simple but touching' open-air service. The music for the hymns, 'For All the Saints', 'O Valiant Hearts' and 'O God, Our Help in Ages Past', was provided by the Keynsham Town Band, some of whom may have led newly enlisted men past the same spot some six years earlier. The 22 names listed at the base of the memorial included Privates Weymouth, Barnett and Mitchell – names from the class of 1902. There must have been many for whom, in the words of Wilfred Owen, every evening had become 'a drawing-down of blinds'.

# Modern Times

$1926$ : ST MARY'S CHURCH sat as it had always done, at the top of the village – like God's own pavilion. But it was no longer alone. The village now had a chapel and a mission hall, started by a couple of firebrand women who thought St Mary's too smart.

> Some few young cottage people who had good voices, and liked to use them, naturally now went to church. So did the old women and men, who had an eye to charity. But the strong, sturdy men, the carters and shepherds stood aloof . . . They cleaned their boots on a Sunday morning while the bells were ringing, and walked down to their allotments, and came home and ate their cabbage, and were as oblivious of the vicar as the wind that blew. They had no present quarrel with the Church; no complaint whatever; nor apparently any old memory or grudge; yet there was something, a blank space as it were, between them and the Church.

This had been written in a different age but it could just as well have been written in 1998. Certainly I never saw any of the men who worked on our house in St Mary's church – not that I blamed them in any way. I was surprised to find myself there and gave Chris the Curate much of the credit for that. It wasn't just that I liked him; I respected him, the more so because I could see that in many ways his was a lonely path. Sunday services would usually end in the church hall (Queen's School as was), drinking cups of coffee in pale green cups and saucers circa 1950. One morning I was chatting with a kindly-faced elderly gentleman who was new to the village. By way of something to talk about I asked him what he thought of Chris's service. There was a pause.

'He's a very good reverend,' he said at last. 'I can see that.'

'I just like the guy, he listens – not many people do that.'

Another thought passed across his face, equally difficult to read but clearly troublesome. He looked at me – suspiciously, before eventually asking: 'Are you a psychiatrist?'

I laughed. 'No, no I'm normal . . . well pretty much.'

'You're a something. I know you are.'

There was nothing new about this. People who lived in manor houses were supposed to be 'a something', traditionally 'a something' who put in the occasional appearance at St Mary's church. Old Lamorock had been a good church man and that, so most of the villagers believed, was the way things ought to be. But in the twentieth century the rules were changing, and for the first time the man 'up at the manor', now another tenant farmer called G.W. Roch, broke with hundreds of years of tradition and worshipped in the Methodist Chapel down in the Shallows. It is possible to see 1926, the year of the General Strike, as the year of the Flowers' Last Stand, for it was then that Major Lamorock, who had chosen to leave Saltford but retained ownership of the house, gave a small patch of land to St Mary's church. This meant that there was now enough land to bury people for the next fifty years.

Electricity came in 1927, refuse collection in 1931 and piped water in 1932. This in turn opened the way for cheaper housing because the services were now all on hand. Houses and shops appeared on either side of the old Bristol–London coaching road – now called a trunk road. The countryside on the edge of built-up areas was increasingly prized – suburban garden estates were springing up all over the place. J.B. Priestley said that the two older versions of England, the country of manor houses and inns (sounds like Saltford) and the cities of iron, steel and railways (sounds like Bristol), were being replaced by a third, 'a new England of arterial and by-pass roads, of filling stations . . . bunga-lows with tiny garages, Woolworth's, motor-coaches, wireless, hiking, factory girls looking like actresses . . . and everything given away with cigarettes and coupons'. Roads became Drives, Lanes or Avenues, and the suburbs became the place to be, offering as they did the best of town and country. To move from a terrace on the edge of Bristol to a bungalow and garage in Saltford, and better still from renting to buying, was a step in the right direction. Half-timbered finishes, bow windows, stained-glass panes, inglenook fireplaces made out of bricks and Gothic front doors, here on either side of the A4 a man could have all this for weekly payments of 12 shillings.

Meanwhile, back at the Manor a pleasant-looking man in his sixties arrived at the front door.

'Good afternoon. Are you Mr Wynn?'

'Yes.'

'I'm Mr Ewins.' We shook hands. There was a pause, no surprise there, but this one was different, he was expecting some response. I smiled in what I hoped he would find a congenial manner, friendly but not too friendly. It must have worked because he continued easily enough.

'I'm pleased to meet you at last. I'm his son.' He waved a grey booklet and looked knowingly over the top of his glasses. The suggestion being that now I had seen the booklet, I would understand. I had learnt that chance meetings like this could often lead to interesting discoveries. Perhaps this mild-mannered man with tortoiseshell glasses was a descendant of William or Walter?

'I'm sorry, I'm not sure I completely follow you.'

'The man who wrote this' – he waved the booklet, was this a clue? 'I'm his son. Haven't you read it?'

'No.'

'You can have a look if you like.'

'I'd really like to, thank you.'

'The only thing I would ask is that you return it, it's a collector's item. Actually we're making a small video about sites of local interest.'

'Great.'

'. . . and we just wondered, if it's not too much trouble, whether we could get a few shots of the house from the front garden?'

As he was speaking two young guys with polished heads and a small video camera wandered up the drive.

'No problem – my pleasure.' I later discovered that he had told them to wait at the bottom of the drive and then, after a few minutes, to stroll up towards the house looking artistic. They managed the first, not sure about the second. I was happy to let them get whatever shots they wanted, and after a quick cup of tea they went on their way, leaving a card: First Video, Keynsham. No project too small, no project too big.

The booklet had been produced by the Saltford Boy Scouts Committee. Dated January 1939 and priced at sixpence, it had been written by C.G. Ewins and contained a small ink etching of a scout holding a Union Jack above the words 'Be Prepared'. 'This booklet is issued in connection with the Saltford Boy Scouts on the occasion of the opening of Saltford Manor House as their headquarters. The Committee desire to acknowledge their deep gratitude to Noel Flower Esq., for his kindness in allowing the free use of his house.'

The scouts had not taken root in Saltford back in 1908 when the movement had started but were now making up for lost time and doing so in style. Led by a Mr Hancock, in January 1939 they struck a deal which allowed them to use the house as their headquarters. Perhaps for the last time the house had a genuine community function but it was not the great and the good who were responsible, it was the young and the willing. For the next six years the scouts were surrounded by frescoes and beams – not bad for one of the county's smaller troops. At the back of the booklet there were a few pages of adverts for the shops that had sprung up in the building boom a few years earlier.

There in the bottom left-hand corner was J.W. Roch, son of G.W. Roch, although the farm referred to was not the Manor. Telephone calls must have been easy – Walter Batstone was 5, J.W. Roch was 95. The old stick telephone with its separate earpiece had been replaced by the all-in-one earpiece and microphone unit and the new models were available in ivory, brown, green, red, silver and gold as well as black. If Walter had wanted to send a last-minute airmail letter he could call Croydon Aerodrome Post Office and dictate his letter over the phone, after which it would be taken down to the hangar and put on the plane. And then there was C.E. Hancock, General Ironmonger alias Scout Master, who sold wood and building materials – an odd-job man who also sold radios. In many houses the radio had replaced the hearth as the focal point of the living room, the point around which all the seating was arranged. There would have been few in Saltford, or anywhere else, who did not hear Neville Chamberlain on 3 September 1939.

> I am speaking to you from the Cabinet Room at 10, Downing Street. This morning the British Ambassador in Berlin handed the German Government a final note, stating that unless we heard from them by 11 o'clock that they were prepared at once to withdraw their troops from Poland a state of war would exist between us. I have to tell you now that no such undertaking has been received and that consequently this country is at war with Germany.

In the years that followed, most people could say exactly where they were at that moment. Churches around the country were full (it was a Sunday). A wireless had been placed in the pulpit at Bath Abbey, the *Bath Chronicle* reporting that the announcement created what they called 'a profound impression'. The next day the BBC rushed out a special copy of the *Radio Times*: 'Broadcasting carries on! That is the slogan of the BBC in this hour of National Endeavour, when the British Nation is nerving itself for the greatest effort it has ever made . . . There will even be a children's hour and regular broadcasts for schools.' In fact *Children's Hour* was cancelled on 4 and 5 September, considered too flippant for such a moment, but was back on Wednesday, 6 September, trimmed down to half an hour but with its original title. *Children's Half-Hour* would, I suppose, have sounded a bit mean.

Every day from then on it was introduced by 'Uncle Mac', who opened up with 'Hello children everywhere', timely words to a country which was engaged in the wholesale evacuation of one and a half million mothers and children from the cities to the country. Paddington, the station which served the West Country, was pandemonium . . . you could not move for people and children, like coming out of a football match. Anyhow, we were put on a train with our luggage, which consisted of a small suitcase. The train was packed with children leaning out of the windows waving to their parents goodbye. Some were crying, as they did not want to leave them; it was a sad sight. I cannot remember if I shed a few tears or not. We did not know if we would see our parents again. The train pulled out of the station and we were on our way to a destination unknown to us at the time.

For just over a hundred children that destination was Saltford. Eight hundred children were bundled out at Bath station with parcel labels hung from their necks. A few mothers had come with them, choosing to say their goodbyes in Bath rather than London, hoping perhaps for the chance to let their guardians know that John slept much better with the door slightly ajar. It was, according to the *Chronicle*, a masterpiece of order. Yes, there were tears, but they were brushed aside. It was the way of things. 'The kiddies are all extremely cheery and one of the accompanying teachers stated that on the journey all had been in the best of spirits.' There is a photo of three boys aged eleven or twelve, shorts, socks finishing just below their knees, caps firmly planted, jackets buttoned three times. The central figure shouldered a bundle of cricketing gear as if it were a rifle – and smiled weakly. The caption read, 'In the hopes of getting a little cricket these London boys brought their stumps, bat and pads with them.' The next day the *Chronicle* reported that some of the children were taking what they described as 'a little time to shake down' but most were enjoying the holiday, whose ending day was yet to be fixed. Either children were different in 1939 or these reports – shot through with a hollow cheerfulness – were missing something. It took a mother to get to the truth.

We are all keeping a check on our emotions. We are a little guarded in what we say for fear of inadvertently annoying people, or straining nerves already taut, or deepening the general depression. We avoid controversy or provocative sallies; what would normally be stimulating arguments might easily sharpen into quarrels just now. One tries to short-circuit emotion rather than share it. The 'genial current of the soul' is dammed up and we fall back on bromides and bright little jokes.

Some of the children were driven away from the station in their guardians' cars in silence, punctuated by bright little jokes; others boarded waiting coaches bound for the surrounding villages – perhaps Saltford got the cricketers.

The children sat cross-legged in Queen's School

being given a sandwich and milk to drink, which really was a luxury for us (having lived all our lives on condensed milk) . . . We were being picked out by all these folks who kept looking us over front and back, I might say. I can remember clinging to my brothers and sisters and saying we were not going to be separated, but they finally came down to the fact that one woman wanted two boys and this dear old lady was there to pick out a girl for her sister. She kept saying she wanted a little girl younger than I was, but anyway she did after all decide that maybe I would do, and that it would be fine because I could see my brothers' house [where they would be staying] from my bedroom window.

Sunday, 10 December. Some three months after they had left London, the Saltford evacuees were dressed in their Sunday best and shipped down to Bath station; they swarmed up the stairs and over the platform. 'When will the train come, Mister?' one eleven-year-old asked the reporter, her brother echoing the question in 'his shrill cockney voice' before darting off in another direction without waiting for an answer. Eventually the train drew into the station, with steam and whistles; more and more of them as they pushed closer, some running alongside the carriages – as well they might, some of them had not seen their parents for three months. 'I had witnessed the arrival of the children three months ago. But the arrival of their parents was a far more moving scene. "I want my mummy," I heard one little girl piteously cry, then suddenly her cry changed as she saw her mummy and ran forward to greet her and daddy as they looked in a rather bewildered fashion about the strange platform.' And then some four hours later, 'Tired, weary but happy the Londoners boarded the long train again,' leaving their children to spend the first Christmas of the war in their new homes.

In the early days it was not uncommon to hear the remark 'It'll all be over by Christmas!' Well, it wasn't, and wouldn't be for another six. But Christmas 1939 was important in spite of, or perhaps because of, the war. People needed to know what they were fighting for and Christmas offered a wonderful opportunity to tell them. The Ministry of Information declared that war or no war, the children of England will not be cheated out of the one day they look forward to all year. 'We're all working, you see, for the same great purpose and it is just as much a crusade – against nations which have no use for Christmas because they have "abolished God" – as that which Christ fought for us . . . Your faith, your laughter and your certainty of good in the end, can make this Christmas as happy as any other.' This article was printed in *Woman's Own* – not the *Church Times*! The government was keen to promote a happy Christmas and provided special trains for those parents separated from their children.

The phrase 'home front' was one of the great phrases of the war, but the home itself was one of the war's first casualties. What happened in Saltford, and in villages all over the country, was an invasion – an invasion of children who now shared bathtubs with those who must have struggled, certainly in the early days, to understand even their accents. That winter, the coldest for fifty years, brought heavy snow and there were snowball fights – not always in the best spirits – between the village boys and the 'vacees', as they were called by the locals. The child population had doubled virtually overnight. Queen's School changed to a shift system, the locals attending in the morning and the 'vacees' in the afternoon.

There were as many different experiences as there were children. Some settled in well, others, like one little girl, were sent to people who were hopelessly unsuitable.

My schoolwork had begun to go down, and teachers had noticed I went very quiet whereas I had been a bit of a chatterbox. The incident that brought things into the open happened when all of a sudden I started menstruating. I had been told by my mother what to expect and what to do if my periods came on, but like girls all over I felt a little scared. I got out of bed one morning to find blood on the sheets, and I went running to tell the lady and to ask for a pad or cloth. All I got was screamed at, called a dirty pig, put into the bedroom, given a cloth, pins and a piece of elastic and told to see to myself . . . The lady berated me all through breakfast, also letting me know she hadn't wanted a girl anyway.

By contrast, those sent to Mrs Roch probably had a wonderful time. The farm had about thirty cows – possibly more given that the pre-war advert had boasted two deliveries per day – and the newcomers may well have helped to cut the grass, taking it in turns to use the short-handled scythe, or collect the chickens' eggs from the long grass which skirted the edges of the fields. Like many farmers' wives, Mrs Roch's husband was away fighting, so she was grateful for the extra help. The evacuees probably learnt how to milk the cows, or perhaps they were sent off to pick rose-hips and blackberries which the Red Cross collected to make jam. Mrs Batstone, a kindly soul, felt sorry for them and sometimes sold them chocolate and broken biscuits at half-price. The boys joined the scouts up at the Manor, the girls knitted socks for the soldiers, and then, in the spring of the following year, Mrs Roch named some of her calves after the children – the ultimate accolade. Haymaking, threshing, mushrooming and nut-collecting – it was a long way from the city.

In July 1940, the southern skies thick with Spitfires and Hurricanes, a new campaign was launched. 'Women of Britain, give us your aluminium . . . We will turn your pots and pans into Spitfires and Hurricanes.' Lord Beaverbrook was getting a bit carried away – he was after all a newspaperman. In fact not many pots and pans were good enough for aircraft production. Nevertheless as a morale-boosting exercise the campaign was a success. Churchill predicted that this would be our 'finest hour' and civilians wanted to do their bit towards the war effort. It was exactly the kind of situation Baden-Powell had in mind in the years leading up to the

First World War. For Saltford, the timing had not been right first time around but now it was. The Saltford troop joined their fellow scouts around the country (now numbering over 400,000) collecting bags of scrap paper, food waste for pigs, rags, bottles, bones for soap and fertiliser, scrap metal and milk bottle tops. The Manor walls, once hung with tapestries and oil paintings, were now covered with posters: 'Save your scrap for the scrap' or 'Waste Littler, Paste Hitler'. The scouts were a scissors-and-paste army who had jumped straight out of the pages of *Boy's Own*.

By the following summer most of the evacuees had returned to London, apart from one London teacher, a Mr Crompton, who decided to stay. The Second World War shifted people around like no other previous event had ever done; everyone's life was affected. The country was full of Mr Cromptons who went somewhere, met someone, did something – not perhaps something of huge national importance but something which changed their own lives from that moment on.

After the landings on the beaches of Normandy in June 1944 the nation waited for what now looked certain to be an Allied victory. It came on 7 May 1945 – and Churchill declared the following day, VE Day, to be a national holiday. It was a sunny day, as well it might be after six years of war, and everyone gathered in clusters in the streets, talking and laughing. A car drove up and down the High Street with two people on the bonnet and one on the roof. There were parties, jelly and blancmange, some tinned grapefruit saved for the day, numerous toasts . . . Churchill (of course), Stalin, Walter Batstone, possibly even one for Mr Crompton and his new fiancée. Outside the Bird in Hand a small gathering listened to one of Mr Hancock's radios which someone had put on an open window ledge. The chimes of Big Ben sounded three o'clock and then, once more, Churchill growled his way out of a Bakelite box – no laughing now, just people standing completely still, caps and hats in hand: that Voice, the voice that had steered them all out of the darkness of 1940 to this present hour, triggering for each person something different; for some it was joy, others sadness, still others disbelief.

No one slept much that night. Mrs Roch remembered the day when war was declared, the day when she and her evacuees had worked in the field and a gust of wind had caught up the hay and carried it far away. The old landmarks had changed; the new ones were not yet clearly defined.

On 15 November 1946, one year after the end of the war, Noel Flower appears to have accepted that it no longer made sense to own a building which neither he nor anyone in his family had lived in for over forty years. The garden and house were given a 1940s make-over – new electrics, cable-knit mustard-coloured wires knitted into the walls (still in evidence when we moved in), new drains and plumbing, and a new kitchen built on at the back.

Children at the beginning of the 1950s still wondered what their parents meant when they spoke about eating oranges, pineapples and chocolate, when they had baths in a few inches of water and wore cheap, threadbare clothes. Walter Batstone had queues outside his shop until July 1954, the date when food rationing finally came to an end. But eventually the mood began to change. There was a young queen on the throne and newspapers and magazines were full of money matters – how much there was of it and how best to spend it.

And so it was that on 24 July 1958, *Country Life*, all antiques and mink coats, published an article about Saltford Manor. The language is that of an old order:

> The lower Avon valley, between Bath and Bristol, has lost none of its charm to an onrush of ribbon development and bungaloid nastiness. For two or three miles east of Keynsham the modern combination of suptopia and roaring traffic is specially dense, disagreeable and hostile to ideas of placid antiquity.

But for all the head-in-the-sand hopelessness of the writer's cause, he correctly identified something about the place.

The article told the story of the house, weaving in and out of Robert, Walter and assorted Lamorocks, bringing the reader up to 1958. 'So it comes about that this ancient dwelling, its central portion a legacy of rare note from the domestic building of eight centuries ago, again conveniently fulfills, in the manner of our own times, the purpose for which it was built.'

'Let's be frank about it,' Harold Macmillan had said the previous summer, summing up what many thought to be a new golden age, 'most of our people have never had it so good. Go around the country . . . and you will see a state of prosperity such as we have never had in my lifetime – nor indeed ever in the history of this country. What is worrying some of us is "Is it too good to be true?" or perhaps I should say "Is it too good to last?"' Saltford certainly had more than its share of that prosperity. People with money came and left in rapid succession, the Manor's final owner being the heiress to Woolworth's. There are tales of surgeons and tailors, television moguls and estate agents; stories of a yellow Bentley in the garage and lawn turf being delivered on silver platters. But Harold Macmillan had been right – it didn't last; the house now belonged to us. We had just bought a second-hand Citroën Spree and were considering some more grass seed. With the all too obvious exception of us, the most significant thing about Saltford during these years was not so much the prosperity of the owners as the length of time any of them stayed. Until 1946 one family had owned this house for 319 years. In the next fifty years it changed hands eleven times. Those who lived here since 1946 were, it seems, restless; nothing seemed to last very long, not least their ability to stay in one place.

By the time we bought the house from the Woolworth's heiress, the water damage caused by the multiple pipe bursts had brought the place to its knees. Restoration specialists had been called in to give their opinions, which they did in expensively bound reports which gave the impression that the building was delicate, that it needed careful handling in order to protect it from further damage. The opposite now seemed to me to be true. Whereas I had thought the work required was radical, I now felt that, with the exception of the strengthening of wall sockets on the large beams on the ground floor, all we had really done was give the place a new set of clothes. In fact the house had probably been similarly redressed many, many times.

Finally, a good word in the circumstances, *our* moment had come – and eight months after buying the place we moved in.

# · 19 ·

# Forever Young

THE ANGLO-SAXONS called the people who lived in Somerset 'Sumorsaete', the people of the summer lands; a good description of us that first summer. William's field had just been mown, bales of roughly stacked hay laid out under freshly laundered skies.

In my memory it was a golden time and yet when I look at the video of Julia's third birthday party, taken two weeks after moving in, I see a little girl I barely know surrounded by other children I definitely don't. Somehow we had managed to persuade what now looks like a collection of strangers to have tea in the garden and to bring their children. The children prowled around each other, sizing each other up, and the parents did much the same thing, the talk endlessly looping around careers and mortgage payments. It was one of those occasions which, were it not for the video, I would have completely forgotten. But it isn't just the people who seem strangers; the house itself feels like a distant memory, somewhere we used to live – austerely beautiful, but cold, with huge expanses of empty white walls. Now, some ten years after moving in, the designer-clean coldness has been replaced by something much warmer.

The story of this house is astonishing not because it is full of drama but rather because it is long; a version of it could be told about any number of places all over England. It had been lived in for nearly a thousand years by people who for the most part were much like us; they just got on with living. It had survived longer than any other house and was therefore distinctive, so distinctive that 16 million people were going to hear about it.

It started with a telephone call. A friendly man from *Country Life* magazine explained that he had found the 1958 article in their archives and wondered if we would like the house to be considered in a competition in their August edition to find Britain's oldest house. I agreed and forgot about the whole thing. About a month later the phone went again – same voice, friendly with now just a hint of excitement, nothing too wild.

'Mr Wynn?'

'Yes.'

'Good morning to you . . . it's *Country Life* here. The new edition has something in it I think you'll find interesting – our expert has decided that Saltford is the winner.'

John Goodall, an eminent architectural historian, had chosen Saltford from a shortlist of seven on the grounds that William's window was similar to work done at Hereford Cathedral – known to have been completed by 1148. In his view this dated Saltford to pre-1150, which made it the oldest inhabited house in Britain. The man from *Country Life* explained that he was putting together a press release and wondered how I would feel about talking to journalists. As an actor I had been spotted on the foothills of fame so that people would stop me and say things like 'I recognise you, you're that bloke off the telly,' or, on one occasion, 'Aren't you the librarian in Burnley?' Let's put it this way, Hugh Grant didn't lose much sleep if he saw my name on the audition list. Nevertheless I did have some experience with the media and felt that I could probably handle whatever interest the article would generate. Indeed, in so far as I thought about it at all, I thought that it might even be fun. I was wrong.

The day before *Country Life* was published, the London *Evening Standard* telephoned and we chatted away for about half an hour. The photographer arrived some twenty minutes later. In the middle of our session the phone went again, this time it was the BBC Radio 4 programme *Today*, wanting to know if they could do a pre-recorded interview to drop into the next morning's programme.

The next day began at about 7.00 a.m. with Anna and me listening to *Today*. The girls came down for breakfast, we had the usual arguments about white or brown toast, during which we wondered how many other people listened to the radio at this time in the morning. It was 7.30. In the next two hours the *Daily Mail*, the *Daily*

*Express*, *The Times*, the *Daily Telegraph*, the *Guardian*, the *Financial Times* and the *Western Daily Press* all called – for the first time. Almost all of them called back another couple of times, some as many as five times. We have two phone lines in the house, one for my office upstairs and one for home downstairs – both rang most of the day.

This was difficult, but not as difficult as a moment later in the morning. The BBC local news sent a crew and reporter, who were followed within minutes by what looked like a cut-price outfit from ITV – less charm, fewer men, no reporter and less equipment. Anna, completely overcome by the avalanche that I appeared to have brought upon us, was hiding with the children in the bedroom. And then, just when I thought things couldn't get any worse, the phone went again.

'Mr Flynn?'

'Wynn.'

'Right . . . Mr Wynn. It's Sky News here.'

'Yes.'

'Sky News.'

'Yes, I understand.'

'Right . . . could we come over to Saltford and do an item for our *Six O'Clock Programme*?'

'Not now.'

'I understand . . . what about in half an hour?'

He was still speaking as I put the receiver down. We unplugged all the land lines – not that it made any difference, somehow they got my mobile number. About half an hour and several calls later a man appeared at the bottom of the drive.

'Mr Wynn?'

'Yes.'

'Sky News.' He handed me a card.

'Sorry, didn't I . . .'

'Yes . . . I know you said you'd prefer us not to come but we were so close. It seemed a shame to turn round and go back.' He sulked around at the bottom of the lawn, made one or two calls on his mobile and eventually shuffled off.

ITV came back at about 5.30 p.m. and set up on the front lawn to do a live feed into their programme. The girls watched it on the

TV in the front room, looking out of the window and back to the screen – an event which gave new meaning to the term 'outside broadcast'. This was followed by a telephone interview with the BBC World Service, our story tagged on behind an earnest item about politics in the Far East. So, what was it about this story that made it suitable for such a programme? In part it may have been because it was a sort of 'star is born' story, featuring an unknown house hauled up from the back row of the chorus. But it appealed, I think, on a deeper level. The house in question wasn't now owned by the National Trust, it was owned by ordinary (very ordinary) people. The *Daily Mail* quoted me as saying, 'A medieval window here, Tudor timbers there. I can look at Norman, Tudor and seventeenth-century architecture before I brush my teeth in the morning. It's strange – in a good way – that we sleep and live in the same rooms where so many families have played out their lives.'

In pursuit of the country dream – the idea that somewhere we could find more space, perhaps a little peace – we had been ambushed. I know now that much of the country dream was just that, a dream, and that dreams are not made by houses, even houses as beautiful as this one. Still it was easier to dream in Saltford Manor than it had been in London. This house is not so much a destination as an embarkation point, available to anyone who sits on a window seat and watches the light close in on a summer's evening. T.E. Lawrence, better known as Lawrence of Arabia, was on to something when he wrote:

> All people dream but not equally. Those who dream by
> night in the dusty recesses of their minds wake in the day
> to find it was vanity: but the dreamers of the day are
> dangerous men for they may act their dreams with open
> eyes, to make it possible.

This house has provided me with a place to dream with open eyes, no better location has ever been given to anyone. I have dreamt my way in and out of a thousand years. If this is dreaming I don't want to wake up.

Julia, on the other hand, didn't want to go to sleep. Flanked by frescoes of Edward the Confessor, the Virgin and Child and a poster of *The Lion King*, she sat up in bed and set off on one of her famously 'difficult' question sessions, saved almost exclusively for the closing moments of the day.

'Will you give me the house when you don't want it any more?'

'I can't say – we'll have to live somewhere.'

'No, I mean when I'm old.'

'Well – you'll have your own house.'

'It won't be so good.'

'You don't know that.'

'I do – it's just . . .' She tried to look brave.

'What?'

'Nothing.'

'No, go on.'

'I don't want it all to change.'

This house has been changed by time and I have been changed by it, for ever.